STORIES WORTH READING

Skills Worth Learning

BOOK 1

BETSY CASSRIEL, SANTA BARBARA CITY COLLEGE

GAIL REYNOLDS, SANTA BARBARA CITY COLLEGE

HEINLE
CENGAGE Learning

Australia • Brazil • Japan • Korea • Mexico • Singapore • Spain • United Kingdom • United States

Stories Worth Reading: Skills Worth Learning Book 1
Betsy Cassriel, Gail Reynolds

Publisher: James W. Brown

Senior Acquisitions Editor: Sherrise Roehr

Director of Product Development:
Anita Raducanu

Associate Development Editor: Tom Jefferies

Editorial Assistant: Katherine Reilly

Director of Product Marketing: Amy Mabley

Product Marketing Manager:
Laura Needham

Senior Field Marketing Manager:
Donna Lee Kennedy

Sr. Production Editor: Maryellen E. Killeen

Technology Manager: Andrew Christensen

Senior Print Buyer: Mary Beth Hennebury

Compositor: Dutton & Sherman Design

Photo Researcher: Dutton & Sherman
Design

Illustrator: Meredith A. Morgan

Cover/Text Designer: Dutton & Sherman
Design

Cover Image: © PINTO/Masterfile

Library of Congress Control Number: 2004116291

ISBN-13: 978-1-4130-0853-1

ISBN-10: 1-4130-0853-4

Heinle
20 Channel Center Street
Boston, MA 02210
USA

Cengage Learning is a leading provider of customized learning solutions with office locations around the globe, including Singapore, the United Kingdom, Australia, Mexico, Brazil, and Japan. Locate your local office at **www.cengage.com/global**

Cengage Learning products are represented in Canada by Nelson Education, Ltd.

Visit Heinle online at **elt.heinle.com**

Visit our corporate website at **www.cengage.com**

Printed in the United States of America
5 6 7 8 9   15 14 13 12 11

FD306

CONTENTS

SCOPE AND SEQUENCE

SKILL BUILDER

Unit #	Topic	Parts	Reading Type	Reading and Word Study Skill Builders
1	All People Big and Small	A Gentle Giant Two Jewels	True Story Website	• Understanding the Main Ideas • Using Your Dictionary • Using *can*
2	Music Magic	Fireworks at the Piano Music for Your Health	True Story Newspaper	• Predicting • Antonyms
3	Old and New Ways	They Dance Like Children The Amish	True Story Essay	• Finding Details • Nouns and Pronouns
4	Healthy Habits	At Home in the Water Eat a Rainbow	True Story Magazine	• Understanding Adverbs of Frequency
5	Learning to Learn	Little Steps, Big Steps Do You Want Better Grades?	True Story Poster	• Simple Past Tense Verb Forms
6	A Friend for Life	Tokyo's Famous Dog Last Lesson for the Graduates	True Story Newspaper	• Adjectives
7	Survival	The Long Rescue Survival Tips	True Story Leaflet	• Imperatives
8	Traveling Across America	Miles for Money Back to Nature Tours	True Story Website	• Using *going to* • Prepositions
9	Fashion Fever	Blue Gold: Levi Strauss Fashion in Harajuku	True Story E-mail	• Using *When*, *What*, and *Where* • Word Groups
10	A Hard Day's Work	The Youngest Executive Job Classifieds	True Story Advertisement	• Making a Timeline

PHOTO CREDITS

Chapter 1
page 3: © Efrem Lukatsky/AP Photo; page 7 (left):
© Briget Jones: The Edge of Reason/Universal;
page 7 (Right): Business Wire/Getty Images; page 7
(bottom): © Jasin Boland/Universal Studios/Bureau
L.A. Collections/Corbis

Chapter 2
page 13 (left): © Reuters/CORBIS; page 13 (right):
© Alyx Kellington/IndexStock; page 14: © Hulton-
Deutsch Collection/CORBIS; page 15: © Lawrence
Lucier/Getty Images; page 20 (Left) © Inc,
MedioImages/IndexStock; page 20 (right) © Roy
Botterell/CORBIS

Chapter 3
page 25 (top):© B.S.P.I./CORBIS; page 25 (bottom):
© Dave Bartruff/CORBIS; page 31 (top) © Chris
Hondros/Staff/Getty Images; page 31 (bottom)
Omni Photo Communications Inc./IndexStock

Chapter 4
page 37: © Gail Mooney/CORBIS; page 39: © David
Gray/Reuters/Corbis; page 43: © Robert
Landau/CORBIS

Chapter 5
page 49: © John Henley/CORBIS; page 51: © Betsy
Cassriel

Chapter 6
page 61 (top left): © The Cover Story/CORBIS; page
61 (top right): © Keyston/Gettyone; page 61 (bottom): © Keyston/Gettyone; © Rob Gage/Taxi/Getty
Images; page 63: © Jeremy Hoare/Alamy; page 69:
© Tom Stewart/CORBIS

Chapter 7
page 73 (left top):© Steve Casimiro/Getty Images;
page 73 (right top): © Joe McBride/Taxi/Getty
Images; page 73 (left bottom): © Royalty-
Free/Corbis; page 73 (right bottom): © Royalty-
Free/Corbis; page 75: © Betsy Cassriel; page 79:
© Getty Images

Chapter 8
page 85: © Chris Minerva/IndexStock; page 87:
© Patricia Starr; page 91 (top): © William A.
Bake/CORBIS; page 91 (middle): © Robert
Glusic/Getty Images; page 91 (bottom): © Franz-
Marc Frei/CORBIS

Chapter 9
page 97 (left): © Pablo Corral V/CORBIS; page 97
(middle): © Hulton-Deutsch Collection/CORBIS;
page 97 (right): © Lawrence Manning/CORBIS; page
99: © AP Photo; page 104 (left): © Peter M.
Wilson/Alamy; page 104 (right): © Nic Cleave
Photography/Alamy

Chapter 10
page 109 (top left): © IndexStock; page 109 (top
middle): © Mark E. Gibson/CORBIS; page 109
(top right): © IndexStock; page 109 (bottom left):
© Royalty-Free/Corbis; page 109 (bottom middle):
© LWA-Dann Tardif/CORBIS; page 109 (bottom
right): © Ruet Stephane/CORBIS SYGMA; page 111:
© Greg Smith/CORBIS

Stories Worth Reading: Skills Worth Learning 1 is a student-centered English language learning textbook containing interesting readings and communicative activities. *Stories Worth Reading: Skills Worth Learning 1* creates an interactive learning environment in which students have opportunities to build not only reading skills but also all-around communicative competence. Themes of courage, perseverance, and empowerment are woven throughout each of the ten units. The text is intended for students at the 500-word level.

STORIES WORTH READING . . .

Stories Worth Reading: Skills Worth Learning 1 contains fresh reading passages relevant to students' lives. The readings range from engaging true stories to articles to web sites and beyond. The text also includes maps and charts to broaden students' reading experiences.

Part One
Part One features a high-interest true story written with controlled vocabulary and sentence structure appropriate to the beginning level. The vocabulary and sentence structure increase in complexity as the book progresses.

Part Two
Part Two includes readings thematically related to Part One. These authentic-like readings (such as newspaper articles, essays, and e-mails) are extensions of the unit topics and help students become familiar with a wide range of reading genres.

. . . SKILLS WORTH LEARNING!

In addition to supporting student learning of appropriate reading skills, *Stories Worth Reading: Skills Worth Learning 1* supports student learning of appropriate reading skills and also builds word study and communication skills.

Reading Skills
Ample practice with good reading skills, such as finding main ideas and details, predicting, and skimming and scanning follows each reading. A wide variety of exercises teach students how to approach different tasks. Pre-reading activities activate students' background knowledge, introduce vocabulary, and relate the unit topic personally to the student.

Word Study Skills
Each unit teaches key vocabulary necessary to understanding each reading and words that are useful for students at this level. Students review words in the original context and practice words in writing and speaking activities.

Skill Builder Feature

Icons throughout the text focus on specific reading and word study skills relevant to students at the beginner level. The Skill Builder feature empowers students with better understanding of and practice with good reading skills. Examples of the reading Skill Builders are: understanding main ideas, finding details, and predicting. In addition, the Skill Builder feature gives students an understanding of and practice with word-study skills. Examples of the word-study Skill Builders are: parts of speech, synonyms and antonyms, prepositions, and dictionary skills.

Communication Skills

Opportunities for developing all-around communicative competence and responding to readings in personally meaningful ways are found after each reading in Communicating Your Ideas. Students interact with one another and with the text through various speaking and writing activities. These engaging activities may involve small group discussion, letter writing, playing games, role-playing, or sharing personal stories. While these activities build fluency and offer practice with vocabulary and grammar, they are also intended to foster an environment of cooperation and community in the classroom.

Synthesis of Skills

The One Step Beyond section at the end of each unit offers exciting suggestions of multi-skill expansion activities to extend learning outside the classroom. There are recommendations for topic-related movies, guest speakers, songs, field trips, and community organizations as well as assignments for journals, interviews, projects, Internet and library research, and more.

A SCIENTIFICALLY-BASED RESEARCH APPROACH

Stories Worth Reading: Skills Worth Learning 1 is based on current, scientifically-based research findings of the most effective means to teach reading skills to adult and young adult learners of English.

Learner-Centered Content

Van Duzer (1999) emphasizes that research on adult ESL students shows that "learners should read texts that meet their needs and are interesting." The readings in *Stories Worth Reading* are carefully selected so that they are both high-interest and relevant to the needs of adults.

Development of Reading Skills and Strategies

Grabe (1995) and Oxford (1990) assert that explicit instruction in reading skills and strategies helps adults improve their reading comprehension. *Stories Worth Reading* integrates explicit reading instruction and highlights key skills using the Skill Builder feature.

Development of New Language

Eskey (1997) emphasizes the importance of adult learners understanding the vocabulary and grammar they encounter as they read. Anderson (1999) suggests that basic vocabulary should be explicitly taught in conjunction with teaching students other strategies for less frequently encountered items. As such, each unit of *Stories Worth Reading* provides word study Skill Builders which demonstrate and offer practice of vocabulary and grammar skills.

Using Background Knowledge

Because research shows that background knowledge facilitates comprehension (Eskey 1997), each unit of *Stories Worth Reading* opens with a photo montage, pictures, discussions, quizzes, and more related to the unit theme.

Anderson, N. (1999). *Exploring Second Language Reading: Issues and Strategies*. Boston: Thomson Heinle.

Eskey, D. (1997). *Models of reading and the ESOL student. Focus on Basics 1 (B)*, 9-11.

Grabe, W. (1995). *Dilemmas for the development of second language reading abilities. Prospect*, 10 (2), 38-51.

Oxford, R.L. (1990). *Language learning strategies: What every reader should know*. Boston: Thomson Heinle.

VanDuzer, C. (1999). *Reading and the Adult Language Learner. ERIC Digest*. Washington D.C.: National Center for ESL Literacy Education.

Getting Ready

Each unit starts with a Getting Ready activity that activates students' background knowledge and stimulates their interest in the topic. Small groups or partners work together in class on these interactive activities.

Pre-reading

Pre-reading activities before each reading prepare students to read. They are communicative and designed to be completed in class before a reading is assigned. Small groups or pairs share their findings with the class.

Reading and Word Study Skills

The readings and their accompanying comprehension and vocabulary exercises can be assigned as homework so that class time is maximized for interaction. In the next class, students can correct exercises, clarify new vocabulary words and their pronunciation, and retell the story. Alternatively, students can do this section in class and discuss the answers to the questions in groups. All of the readings are available on the audio tape and CD that accompany this text.

Skill Builders

Teacher and students work together in class to build understanding and practice the reading and word skills presented in Skill Builders.

Communicating Your Ideas

Communicating Your Ideas activities help students relate story themes to themselves and to others, exploring their ideas about the topic and building fluency. There are various speaking activities, which can be done in small groups and pairs. Students can do the **Write About It** writing assignments as homework and then share with classmates. The reading passages and follow-up activities act as prewriting exercises for the writing activities.

For the **Talk About It** discussion questions, students should be in groups of three or four, sitting in a circle facing one another. Cooperative learning groups, in which students are assigned roles, work well. For a group of four students, the roles might be discussion leader, spokesperson, recorder, and timekeeper. Groups report back to the class with the help of graphic organizers, such as newsprint, transparencies, charts, drawings, etc. We have great success keeping students in the same groups or "teams" for several weeks and even an entire semester. For any group activity, keep in mind that groups may be formed randomly, by student choice, or teacher choice, according to your objectives.

One Step Beyond activities can be plugged in at any point in each unit. In fact, many of these activities are assignments that may take students a week or more to complete. Some take advance planning on the teacher's part. We suggest that as a teacher becomes familiar with the text at the beginning of the semester, he/she reads all of the One Step Beyond pages immediately. Then he/she can take advantage of these opportunities by planning ahead of time. These activities can be completed by the entire class, in small groups, with partners, or as individuals. We've had wonderful success in our classes giving students a number of different choices from the One Step Beyond lists and then having students share presentations with the class.

ACKNOWLEDGMENTS

The publisher would like to thank the following individuals who offered helpful feedback and suggestions on the text:

Mona Brantley
Des Moines Area Community College,
Des Moines, IA

Janeece Docal
Bell Multicultural Senior High School,
Washington, DC

Diane Frangie
Fordson High School, Dearborn, MI

Virginia Guleff
Miramar College, San Diego, CA

Arnulfo Lopez
Delano High School, Delano, CA

Dr. Karen Morante
LaSalle University/BUSCA, Philadelphia, PA

The authors thank Sherrise Roehr for understanding and believing in our project and Tom Jefferies for embracing our vision, adding his own wonderful ideas, and focusing an otherwise untamed work.

Thanks go to Rene Mireles, Geoff Godfrey, and Patricia Starr who generously shared their life stories with us and enthusiastically supported the project. Thanks go to Marit ter-Mate Martinsen for her great input and to Leona, friends, and family.

This book is lovingly dedicated to Wayne, Christopher, and baby Brian.

ALL PEOPLE
BIG AND SMALL

GETTING READY

1. Ask your partner the questions.

    What's your name?
    Where are you from?

2. Walk around your classroom with your partner. Introduce your partner to other students.

    Example: *This is Phillipe. He is from France.*

A GENTLE GIANT

PRE-READING

Look at the pictures below. Talk about them with your partner. Write new words next to the pictures. Then listen to your teacher read the story.

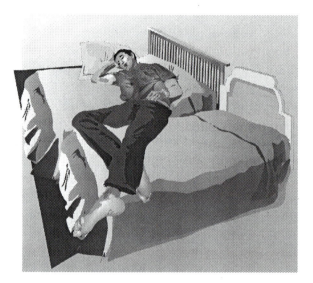

A GENTLE GIANT

Leonid Stadnik is very tall. He is 8 feet 4 inches. Leonid is not a child. He is 33 years old, but he is still growing. He is growing because he has an unusual medical condition. Leonid is sad. Leonid doesn't like being tall, but his doctor says, "Leonid, you will get taller!" Leonid lives in a small village in Ukraine. He cannot leave his village. He cannot go on a bus. He is too tall and heavy. He weighs 440 pounds. He says, "Riding on a bus is like getting into a trunk of a car."

Leonid lives with his mother in a small house. He cannot stand up straight in the house. He sleeps on two beds put together to make one long bed. His feet are very big. They are 17 inches long. He needs expensive shoes. Leonid does not have much money. Leonid is a veterinarian, but he cannot work now. His friends help him buy shoes.

He tries to stay busy. He helps his mother with their cows and pigs. He has a tiny pet parakeet. Leonid is a very kind man. He has many friends in the village. Leonid's friends want to take him on a trip. They want to show him the tall Carpathian Mountains. They tell him, "The mountains are taller than you!"

READING AND WORD STUDY SKILLS

A. Understanding the Main Ideas

SKILL BUILDER

Every paragraph has a main idea. The main idea is the most important idea of a paragraph. The main idea is often the first sentence of a paragraph.

Complete the sentences with the correct words.

1. Leonid is _____.
   a. short   b. growing   c. taking the bus

2. Leonid has a strange _____.
   a. medical condition   b. house   c. pet

3. Leonid's friends like him because _____.
   a. he is poor   b. he is tall   c. he is kind

4. Leonid's life is _____.
   a. easy   b. difficult   c. happy

B. Finding Details

There is one mistake in each sentence. Correct it.

1. Leonid is ~~6~~ ⁸feet 4 inches tall.

2. He lives in a big village in Ukraine.

3. Leonid lives with his father in a small house.

4. Leonid is a teacher, but he can't work now.

5. Leonid's neighbors want to take him on a trip.

Complete Leonid's information form.

INFORMATION FORM

Name:_____ Height:_____

Nationality:_____ Weight:_____

Occupation:_____*veterinarian*_____ Age:_____

C. Learning New Words

Match the word to a definition or picture.

1. _____ weighs
2. _____ heavy
3. _____ busy
4. _____ kind
5. _____ village
6. _____ growing

a.

b. a very small town
c. to have a lot of things to do
d. having a lot of weight
e.

f. friendly or helpful

D. Using New Words

Complete the sentences. Use words from exercise C.

1. A city is a big place. A _____ is very small.

2. Pete likes to help people. He gives them a lot of his time. He is very
   _____.

3. Can you help me? These books are _____.

4. Victor has classes all day, and then he works at night. He is very
   _____.

5. My son Christopher is _____. His pants are too small now!

E. Using *can*

SKILL
BUILDER

1. We use *can* to talk about ability. We use *cannot* or *can't* when we do not have the ability.

   Examples: *Ari loves music. She <u>can play</u> the guitar.*
                 Brian is a baby. He <u>can't walk</u>.

2. Complete the sentences with *can* or *can't*.

   a. Leonid _____ stop growing.

   b. Leonid _____ ride in a bus.

   c. Leonid _____ take care of his parakeet.

   d. Leonid _____ leave his village.

   e. Leonid _____ help his mother.

   f. Leonid _____ sleep in a regular bed.

3. Ask your partner: What can you do? What can't you do?

4. Write sentences about you and your partner. Use *can* and *can't*. Then share your sentences with your class.

   Example: *I can dance.*
                Julia can't type.

   _____

   _____

   _____

COMMUNICATING YOUR IDEAS

A. Write About It

1. Complete the information form with your information.

```
┌─────────────────────────────────────────────────────────────┐
│                    INFORMATION FORM                          │
│                                                              │
│   Name:_____       Age:_____           │
│                                                              │
│   Nationality:_____    Marital Status:_____      │
│                                                              │
│   Occupation:_____     Address:_____        │
│                                                              │
│   Height:_____     Phone Number:_____        │
│                                                              │
└─────────────────────────────────────────────────────────────┘
```

B. Talk About It

Ask a partner the questions. Complete the form with his or her information. Use the questions below:

What is your name?   *How old are you?*
What is your nationality?   *Are you married, divorced or single?*
What is your occupation?   *What is your address?*
How tall are you?   *What is your phone number?*

```
┌─────────────────────────────────────────────────────────────┐
│                    INFORMATION FORM                          │
│                                                              │
│   Name:_____       Age:_____           │
│                                                              │
│   Nationality:_____    Marital Status:_____      │
│                                                              │
│   Occupation:_____     Address:_____        │
│                                                              │
│   Height:_____     Phone Number:_____        │
│                                                              │
└─────────────────────────────────────────────────────────────┘
```

TWO JEWELS

PRE-READING

1. Talk with a small group.

   a. Do you like movies? What kind of movies do you like?

   b. What are some of your favorite movies? Who are your favorite actors?

2. Look at the movie photos. Match a word in the box to a picture.

___animation   ___romantic comedy   ___action/adventure

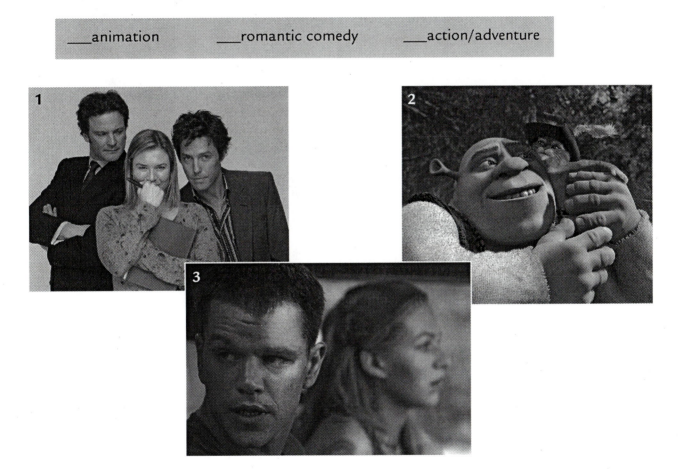

3. What is a movie review? Do you read movie reviews? Why? Read the review of *Two Jewels* on the next page. Would you like to see this movie?

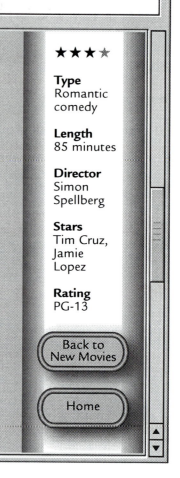

Address: http://www.moviereviews.com

★ ★ ★ ☆

NEW MOVIE REVIEWS

Two Jewels

Do you like laughing? Then go and see *Two Jewels*. It stars Tim Cruz and Jamie Lopez. Lopez plays a **rich** tennis star. Someone steals her diamonds. Cruz is a kind police officer. He is the hero. He tries to find the jewel thief. They don't find the diamonds, but they find love!

Two Jewels is a **funny** movie. It's funny because Cruz and Lopez are very different. Cruz is **quiet**. He does not say very much. Lopez is **talkative**. She is always talking and joking. Cruz wears a gray suit most of the time. Lopez wears **elegant** clothes and expensive jewelry. Cruz has short, brown hair and blue eyes. Lopez has long, blonde hair and beautiful green eyes.

The director Simon Spellberg has made a beautiful comedy. *Two Jewels* is a real gem.

Type
Romantic comedy

Length
85 minutes

Director
Simon Spellberg

Stars
Tim Cruz, Jamie Lopez

Rating
PG-13

Back to New Movies

Home

READING AND WORD STUDY SKILLS

A. Understanding the Main Ideas

Circle T for true or F for false.

1. *Two Jewels* is a funny movie.   T   F

2. Tim Cruz and Jamie Lopez are the same.   T   F

3. The reviewer likes the movie.   T   F

4. A thief steals some diamonds.   T   F

B. Finding Details

1. Check (✔) the correct box.

	Tim Cruz	Jamie Lopez
a. is a police officer.	☐	☐
b. is a tennis star.	☐	☐
c. has short brown hair.	☐	☐
d. has long blond hair.	☐	☐
e. has green eyes.	☐	☐
f. has blue eyes.	☐	☐

2. Write the answer.

a. What type of movie is it? _____

b. How long is the movie? _____

c. Who is the director? _____

d. Who are the stars? _____

e. What is the rating? _____

C. Learning New Words

Unscramble the words. Then draw a line from the word to its definition.

1. eleantg _____   a. having a lot of money

2. stale _____   b. very beautiful and graceful

3. crih _____   c. to see or discover something

4. dnif _____   d. to take something that is not yours

D. Using New Words

Draw a line to complete each sentence.

1. I am trying to find   a beautiful house.

2. The rich woman has   to the party.

3. Sometimes people steal   my car keys.

4. Maria is wearing an elegant dress   bicycles from school.

E. Using Your Dictionary

1. Using your dictionary helps you learn new words. A dictionary gives the *pronunciation* of the word, *definitions* of the word and *example sentences* using the word.

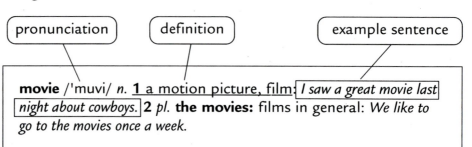

$\boxed{\text{pronunciation}}$ $\boxed{\text{definition}}$ $\boxed{\text{example sentence}}$

movie /ˈmuvi/ *n.* **1** a motion picture, film: *I saw a great movie last night about cowboys.* **2** *pl.* **the movies:** films in general: *We like to go to the movies once a week.*

2. *Jewel* and *hero* are two words from the reading above. Look at the dictionary entries. Draw lines to the parts of each entry like the example above.

$\boxed{\text{pronunciation}}$ $\boxed{\text{definition}}$ $\boxed{\text{example sentence}}$

jewel /ˈdʒuəl/ *n.* **1** a precious or semi-precious gemstone: *Diamonds, rubies, and emeralds are beautiful jewels.*

$\boxed{\text{pronunciation}}$ $\boxed{\text{definition}}$ $\boxed{\text{example sentence}}$

hero /ˈhɪroʊ/ *n.* **-roes 1** the main character in a novel, film, play, etc: *The hero in the movie saved the world.*

COMMUNICATING YOUR IDEAS

A. Talk About It

Work with a partner. Describe the people in the pictures. Use the words in the box.

Example: *Natasha has long hair. Tony has a goatee.*

short	short hair	moustache	big eyes
tall	thin	older	small eyes
long hair	heavy	goatee	young

B. Write About It

Write about someone in your class. Keep the person's name a secret. Read your description to your classmates. They will guess who you are describing.

Example: *She is young. She is tall. She is Thai and she is single. She has dark brown hair and brown eyes. Her hair is long. She has a pink blouse. She is friendly. Who is she?*

_____

_____

_____

ONE STEP BEYOND

■ **Internet or Library**

Work with your class or with a partner. Find the *Guinness Book of World Records*. Who is the shortest person in the world? How short is he? Who is the oldest man in the world? The oldest woman? How old are they?

■ **Encyclopedia**

Look in a world encyclopedia. Talk to someone from Ukraine. Find out some facts about Ukraine. Where is it? What is the population? What language do people speak there?

■ **Photos**

Bring a photo of a person in your family. Write a short description of the person. Share them with your class.

■ **Movie**

Watch *Gulliver's Travels* about a giant. Draw a picture and describe Gulliver.

■ **In Your Journal**

Write a description of a friend or family member. Use words you learned in this unit. Or write about your favorite movies.

■ **CNN**

Watch the CNN® video clip for this unit.

MUSIC MAGIC

GETTING READY

1. Look at the pictures. Do you know the musicians? What kind of music are they playing? Do you like this music?

2. Check (✓) the correct box.

Do you like...?	Yes, it's great!	It's okay.	No, it's awful!
Pop	☐	☐	☐
Rock	☐	☐	☐
Hip-hop	☐	☐	☐
Classical	☐	☐	☐
Jazz	☐	☐	☐
Traditional	☐	☐	☐
Country	☐	☐	☐
Other: _____	☐	☐	☐

3. Work with a partner. Ask your partner about music.

Example: *"Do you like pop music?"*
             "Yes, it's great!"

PART ONE

FIREWORKS AT THE PIANO

PRE-READING

SKILL BUILDER

Predicting

Predicting means to guess. When we predict, we think about what will happen. Predicting is a good reading skill. Predicting shows you what to expect before you read. It also helps you to guess new vocabulary and read faster.

1. Read the definition of "fireworks" from the *Newbury House Dictionary of American English*. Do you like fireworks? When do you see them? How do they make you feel?

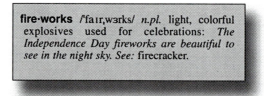

fire·works /ˈfaɪrˌwɜrks/ *n.pl.* light, colorful explosives used for celebrations: *The Independence Day fireworks are beautiful to see in the night sky. See:* firecracker.

2. What is the title of the reading? Look at the photo below. What is happening? Does the audience like the music?

3. Look at the picture of the musician on page 15. What do you think the story is about?

FIREWORKS AT THE PIANO

Lang Lang is 24 years old. He is from Shen Yang, China. He plays piano and he is famous. He is happy today because the audience liked his concert very much.

Lang Lang started studying piano when he was three years old. Today, he gives concerts all over the world. He plays in Paris, Vienna, Chicago, Berlin, New York and other places. A few years ago, he played for 8,000 people in Beijing, China. He plays classical music by Mozart, Brahms, Tchaikovsky and others. He also likes to play traditional Chinese music.

Lang Lang's father is a well-known Chinese musician. He plays a Chinese instrument called an *er-hu*. Lang Lang usually plays concerts alone, but sometimes his father plays with him. They played together in a concert for the first time on Father's Day. The audience loved it.

Lang Lang likes to play video games and ping pong in his free time. He likes to watch the American golfer Tiger Woods and the Chinese basketball player Yao Ming on television.

It is very exciting to watch Lang Lang play piano. He bounces on his piano stool when he plays. Sometimes he throws his arms up in the air when he finishes playing. The audience cheers. Lang Lang says, "I just love to play. It's never boring. It's always new." He says that playing the piano is like electrical energy. His audiences can feel his energy. It is like fireworks!

READING AND WORD STUDY SKILLS

A. Understanding the Main Ideas

Circle the correct word(s) to complete each sentence.

1. Lang Lang plays _piano/violin_.

2. He is _old/young_.

3. He is _exciting/boring_ to watch.

4. Lang Lang gives concerts _in China only/all over the world_.

B. Finding Details

Circle the correct answer.

1. A few years ago, Lang Lang played for _____ people in Beijing, China.

   a. 800   b. 8,000

2. Lang Lang's father plays _____.

   a. piano   b. a traditional Chinese instrument

3. Lang Lang and his father played a concert together for the first time on _____.

   a. Father's Day   b. his birthday

4. Lang Lang's piano playing is like _____.

   a. fireworks   b. boring

5. Lang Lang started studying piano when he was _____.

   a. three years old   b. three months old

6. Lang Lang likes to play _____.

   a. basketball   b. ping pong

C. Learning New Words

Complete the sentences with the words below.

audience	famous	exciting	free time
watch	piano		

1. Lang Lang plays the _____.

2. The _____ likes his concerts very much. The concerts are very _____.

3. Lang Lang likes to play ping pong in his _____.

4. He also likes to _____ basketball on television.

5. Everybody knows Lang Lang in China. He is _____.

D. Using New Words

Complete the questions. Use a word from exercise C. Then ask your partner the questions.

1. Do you like to _____ television?

2. What do you do in your _____?

3. Do you know someone _____?

4. Can you play the _____?

5. Do you like to sing for an _____?

6. Do you think basketball is an _____ sport?

E. Antonyms

SKILL BUILDER

Antonyms are words with opposite meanings. *Cold* and *hot* are antonyms.

1. Write the missing letters to find antonyms from the story.

a. start   f __ __ __ s h

b. sad   __ __ p p __

c. new   __ __ d

d. boring   __ x __ __ __ i n g

e. apart   t __ g __ __ __ e __

f. always   n __ __ __ __

2. Write sentences. Use the antonyms from Exercise E.

Examples: *I always eat chocolate in the afternoon.*
             My car is old.

_____

_____

_____

_____

_____

_____

COMMUNICATING YOUR IDEAS

A. Talk About It

Talk with a group about the questions below. Then complete the chart.

1. Do you play a musical instrument? If yes, what? What instrument would you like to learn to play?

2. Do you like to sing? If yes, what do you sing? When and where do you sing?

3. Do you like to go to concerts? Why?

4. What kind of music do you listen to? Who are your favorite bands or singers? Why?

Name	1. Instrument	2. Sing	3. Concerts	4. Music
Ari	guitar	yes	sometimes	Celine Dion

B. Interviewing

1. Lang Lang likes to play ping-pong and video games in his free time.
   Look at the pictures. Write the names of the activities.

			Other:
listening to music			

2. Ask your classmates the question.

   "What do you like doing in your free time?"
   "I like _____."

C. Write About It

Write sentences about you. Then write sentences about your classmates.
Share your sentences with your class.

Examples: *I like playing basketball.*
  Mario likes listening to romantic music.

1. _____

2. _____

3. _____

4. _____

5. _____

MUSIC FOR YOUR HEALTH

PRE-READING

Look at the pictures. Where is the young man? What is he playing? How do you think he feels? Where is the woman? What is she doing? How do you think she feels?

Do you play a musical instrument? How does playing or listening to music make you feel?

MUSIC FOR YOUR HEALTH
by Dr. Mary Melody

I am a doctor. People often come to see me because they have colds or coughs. People also come to see me because they are sad, stressed or depressed. Sometimes talking helps. Sometimes medicine helps. But many doctors think that music can help people feel better. I asked a few of my patients how music helps them.

"Sometimes I was **angry** when I was a child. My family said, 'Play your feelings on the piano!' Sometimes I play a loud song on the piano. Soon I feel **calm**. I can laugh and **cry** through my fingers on piano. It's natural for me. It's like breathing."

"Listening to music helps me relax. It clears my mind. It makes me feel positive. I like to listen to music and dance when I clean my house."

"I play the flute. I like playing at night when it is quiet. If I am **stressed**, I can play my flute. I **forget** my problems. I only feel the music. After playing I am **tired** and I am **happy**. I always sleep well after playing my flute."

Are you a musician? Good! Keep playing. If you are not a musician, listen to music and sing or dance. It's good medicine.

READING AND WORD STUDY SKILLS

A. Understanding the Main Ideas

Write T for true or F for false.

1. _____ Music is good for you.

2. _____ Music makes people angry.

3. _____ Music helps people feel better.

4. _____ You need to play piano or flute to relax.

B. Finding Details

Circle the correct answer to complete the sentence.

1. The flute player _____ after playing the flute.

    a. feels bad   b. sleeps well

2. Another patient listens to music and dances when _____.

    a. she cooks dinner   b. she cleans the house

3. The pianist's family said _____.

    a. "Play your feelings on the piano."   b. "Go play outside!"

C. Learning New Words

Write the correct word below each picture.

stressed	calm	angry

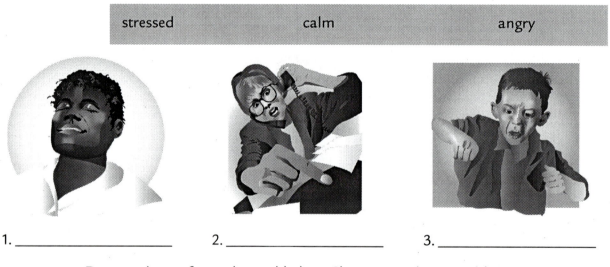

1. _____   2. _____   3. _____

Draw a picture for each word below. Share your pictures with a partner.

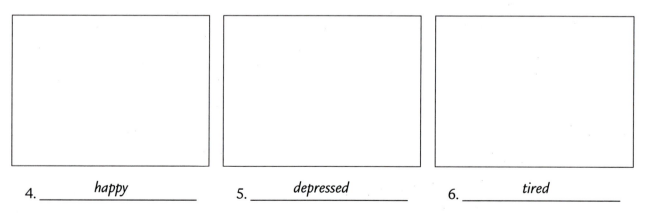

4. _____*happy*_____   5. _____*depressed*_____   6. _____*tired*_____

D. Using New Words

Draw a line to connect the sentences.

1. It's a beautiful day today.   She is stressed.

2. I need a nap.   His parents are angry.

3. Aki hit her brother.   I am happy.

4. Josef lost his job.   we feel calm.

5. Sonia is very busy.   I am tired.

6. When we listen to soft music,   He is depressed.

COMMUNICATING YOUR IDEAS

A. Talk About It

Talk about the questions with a small group.

1. What makes you happy?

2. What makes you stressed?

3. What makes you angry?

4. What makes you calm?

B. Write About It

How do you feel today? Write four sentences about you. Share some with your class.

Example: *I feel happy today.*
             I don't feel stressed.

1. _____

2. _____

3. _____

4. _____

C. Role Play

Work with a partner. Think of a situation when you feel happy, stressed, calm or tired. Write a dialogue. Act it out for the class.

■ **Internet Research**

Look for some photos of Lang Lang on the Internet. Then look for a website about your favorite musician or composer. Find pictures of him or her to share with your class. Tell why you like the musician.

■ **Music Presentation**

Bring a recording of your favorite music or musician. Play a short piece of music for your class. Explain why you like the music. Or, teach your classmates how to do a dance, play an instrument or sing a song.

■ **Free-time Poster**

Find or draw pictures of your favorite free time activities. Make a poster. Show it to the class.

■ **Movies**

Watch a video. Some movies you might like to watch are *Fantasia*, *The Sound of Music* or *Sweet Dreams*. Write your feelings about the movie and the music in your journal.

■ **In Your Community**

Find a free concert in your community. Go with a friend. Tell your class about your experience. What did you like about the concert? How did you feel listening to the music?

■ **In Your Journal**

When do you listen to or play music? What do you listen to or play? How does it make you feel? Write about it in your journal.

■ **CNN.**

Watch the CNN® video clip for this unit.

OLD AND NEW WAYS

GETTING READY

1. Look at the picture. Who is in the picture? What are they wearing?
   What are they doing?

2. What is in the picture? Where are the people? Why?

THEY DANCE LIKE CHILDREN

PRE-READING

Work with a partner. Talk about each picture below. Listen to your teacher read the story.

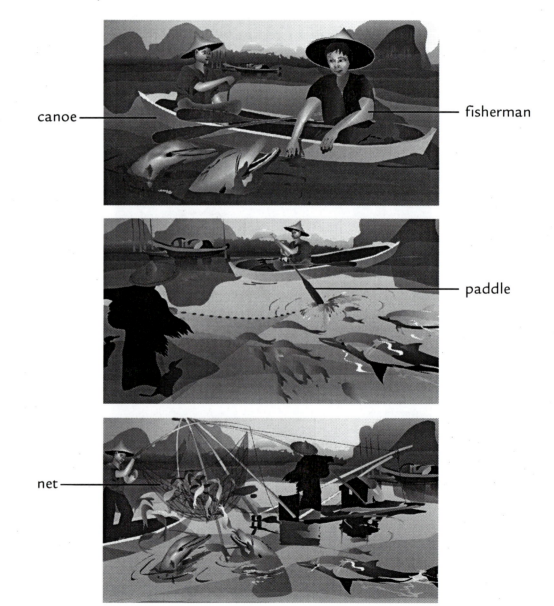

canoe

fisherman

paddle

net

THEY DANCE LIKE CHILDREN

Myint Kyaw Oo and his family are fishermen. They live in Myanmar. Myanmar is in Asia. They fish in the Ayeyarwady River. They catch fish in an unusual way. Some special friends help them. The special friends are dolphins. Young Myint Kyaw Oo's father, grandfather and great-grandfather all fish with dolphins.

The fishermen and the dolphins work together. First, the fishermen call the dolphins. The fishermen hit the side of the canoe like a drum. The dolphins swim near the boat. Then the fishermen hit the water with a canoe paddle. They also make noise with their nets on the boat. Two female dolphins push a school of fish to the canoe. When the fish are close to the canoe, the fishermen throw their nets into the water. Then the fishermen are ready to pull their nets into the canoe. The nets are full of fish!

The fishermen and the dolphins can't catch all of the fish. Some fish do not go in the net. These fish swim away. The dolphins eat these fish!

The fishermen love the dolphins. They like to watch the dolphins swim and play in the water. They say that the dolphins dance like children.

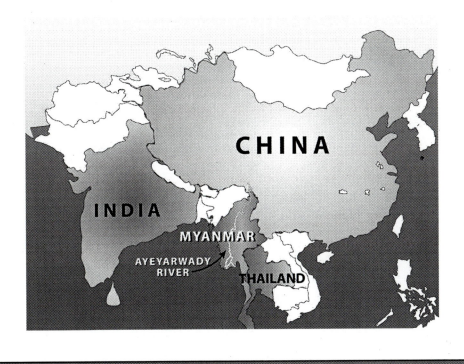

READING AND WORD STUDY SKILLS

A. Understanding the Main Ideas

1. Circle the main idea of the story.

   Myanmar
   Fishing with Dolphins
   Dolphins

2. Put the sentences into the correct order.

   a. _____ The dolphins eat fish.

   b. _____ Two dolphins move the fish into the nets.

   c. __1__ The fishermen call the dolphins.

   d. _____ The fishermen throw their nets into the water.

   e. _____ The fishermen pull their nets into the canoe.

B. Finding Details

SKILL BUILDER

A paragraph often has many *details*. Details tell more about the main ideas. A detail is specific information or examples.

Draw a line to make complete sentences.

1. Myint Kyaw Oo and his family live in	do not go in the net.
2. The fishermen hit the water	with a canoe paddle.
3. Some fish	the dolphins swim and play.
4. The fishermen love to watch	Myanmar.

C. Learning New Words

Write the missing letters to complete the antonyms from the story.

1. pull   __ __ s h

2. far   c l o __ __

3. throw   c __ __ c h

4. empty   f __ __ __

5. common   u n __ __ __ __ __

6. male   f e __ __ __ __

D. Using New Words

Complete the sentences with the correct words from exercise C.

1. The glass is _____ of milk. Please drink it.

2. A sign on the door said "pull." The other side said "_____."

3. I live _____ to school. I walk there in five minutes.

4. _____ the ball!

5. Is the dog male or _____?

6. Rain is _____ in the desert.

COMMUNICATING YOUR IDEAS

A. Talk About It

Talk about the following questions with a small group.

1. Do you like fishing? How do you fish?

2. Do you like to eat fish? How often do you eat fish?

3. Do fishermen in other parts of the world catch fish in the same way as in Myanmar? How do fishermen catch fish in other parts of the world?

4. Do other animals help people work? What animals?

5. The fishermen of Myanmar fish in a traditional way. What do you do in a traditional way?

B. Reading a Map

1. The fishermen of Myanmar catch fish in a traditional way with dolphins. All over the world, people use animals to work in traditional ways. Look at the map below. What other animals work with people? Where?

2. Work with your group. Write the number from the map next to the correct sentence.

   a. _____ In Africa, camels carry people and things.

   b. _____ In Australia, dogs take care of sheep.

   c. _____ In South America, llamas carry things for people.

   d. _____ In Asia, elephants pull logs for people.

   e. _____ In Europe, horses pull wagons and carts.

   f. _____ In North America, cats catch mice.

3. What modern ways can people use instead of these animals? Why do you think they use animals and not modern ways?

THE TRADITIONAL LIFE OF THE AMISH

PRE-READING

Look at the photos. Who are the people in the pictures? What are they doing? What are they wearing? Where do they live?

Tara's class is studying traditional cultures. Read her report about the Amish.

THE AMISH
BY TARA DOMBROWOSKI

Who are the Amish?

The Old Order Amish is a religious group in the United States. Amish people don't live like people in the modern world. They don't use modern things like cars, televisions and washing machines. There are about 180,000 Old Order Amish people. Many live in Ohio, Indiana, Illinois and Pennsylvania.

How do the Amish live?

These Amish people live on family farms. They do not use tractors. They use horses and wagons. They have farm animals, and they grow food. The women wash clothes by hand. Amish people have no computers or telephones. They communicate with friends by visiting and writing letters. The Amish do not have radios or CD players.

What is an Amish house like?

Amish houses do not have electricity. They do not use microwaves or coffee makers. Some use gas power for stoves, refrigerators and hot water. Many Amish do not have sinks and toilets with running water in their kitchens and bathrooms. The Amish make their own furniture. They make beautiful tables, chairs, beds and cabinets for their houses.

What do the Amish wear?

Amish people wear simple clothes. An Amish man usually wears a dark suit with a hat and black shoes. Married men have beards but no moustaches. An Amish woman usually wears a dress with a long skirt. She does not cut her hair. She wears it in a bun.

My Thoughts

I am surprised people live like this in the United States. It is very interesting. I would like to visit Amish country.

A. Understanding the Main Ideas

Circle the correct answer.

1. The Amish are _____.
   a. a religious group   b. a school

2. The Amish do not use _____.
   a. horses   b. many modern things

3. Amish people live _____.
   a. on farms   b. in cities

B. Finding Details

1. Draw a line from the main idea to the detail.

   a. Amish do not use electricity.

   They make tables, chairs, beds and cabinets.

   b. Amish people make their own furniture.

   An Amish kitchen does not have a microwave oven or coffee maker.

   c. Amish people wear simple clothes.

   Men usually wear dark suits with black or straw hats and black shoes.

2. Put a check next to the things the Old Order Amish use.

   ___ horses   ___ electricity   ___ cars

   ___ beds   ___ televisions   ___ chairs

   ___ letters   ___ CD players   ___ wagons

   ___ washing machines   ___ computers   ___ telephones

   ___ refrigerators   ___ radios

C. Learning New Words

Complete the sentence. Draw a line to the correct word.

1. The Amish live on _____.   a. modern

2. They are _____.   b. farms

3. They don't use _____ things.   c. wear

4. Amish people _____ simple clothes.   d. religious

D. Nouns and Pronouns

A noun is a person, place or thing. *New York, student* and *computer* are all nouns. Pronouns are words that take the place of nouns. Subject pronouns are *I, you, he, she, it, we* and *they*.

Example: *Timothy lives on a farm.* He *has horses, cows, pigs and chickens.*

My parents are coming to visit me. They *are arriving on Thursday.*

Circle the pronoun. Then draw an arrow from the underlined noun to its pronoun.

1. The Amish do not use cars. They drive horses and buggies.

2. Amish houses are simple. They do not have electricity.

3. An Amish kitchen is not modern. It does not have a microwave oven, dishwasher or toaster.

4. An Amish woman usually wears a dress with a long skirt. She does not cut her hair.

Put the nouns in the box into the correct columns.

tractor	the United States	women	telephone
the Amish	refrigerator	friends	Pennsylvania

people	places	things

COMMUNICATING YOUR IDEAS

A. Talk About It

Talk about the questions with a small group.

1. Do you like to cook food with a stove or a microwave oven?

2. Do you like to wash dishes by hand or use a dishwasher?

3. Do you like to write letters or e-mails?

4. Do you like to watch television or read books?

5. Would you like to live like the Amish? What would you like about it? What would you not like about it?

B. Write About It

Write sentences about your ways. How do you like to do things?

Example: *I like washing dishes by hand.*
            I don't like using a dishwasher.

_____

_____

_____

_____

_____

_____

ONE STEP BEYOND

■ **Library or Internet**
Look up the Amish on the Internet or in the library. Find photos. Share them with your class.

■ **Research**
Find information about animals that help people. Make a list. How do they help people? Where in the world do they live?

■ **Movies**
Watch *The Gods Must Be Crazy*. What new and old ways do people use in the movie?

■ **Design a House**
Work with a team. Draw your dream house. Is it modern or traditional? Write the names of the rooms and furniture, etc. Have a contest and vote on the best house design.

■ **In Your Journal**
Write about your life today. Is it the same or different from your life in the past? Use new vocabulary words you learned from this unit.

■ **CNN.**
Watch the CNN® video clip for this unit.

HEALTHY HABITS

GETTING READY

Walk around your classroom. Ask your classmates the questions below. When someone answers "yes," write the name in the box.

Do you...?	Name	Name
usually wake up early		
always eat breakfast		
like to run		
sometimes go to bed late		
like to swim		
exercise often		
eat a lot of fruits and vegetables		

Share your answers with the class.

AT HOME IN THE WATER

PRE-READING

The story below is about Michael Phelps. He is a famous Olympic swimmer. Look at the pictures and talk about what he does every day. Listen to your teacher read the story.

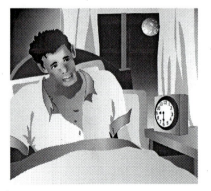

AT HOME IN THE WATER

Every day, Michael Phelps wakes up early. At 7:00, he goes to the pool near his house for swim practice. He swims a lot. He often swims 7,000 or 8,000 meters in the morning. After swimming, Michael stretches and does some exercises. He needs to be careful. He never runs or lifts weights because he could hurt himself. Michael's body is perfect for swimming, but not for moving on land. He

is 6 feet 4 inches tall. He weighs 195 pounds. He has an extra long body and extra long arms. He has short legs. He has big feet like the flippers of a fish.

After swim practice Michael goes to school, but he is hungry! Before school, he and his swim partner eat breakfast at a favorite restaurant. Michael has fried egg sandwiches, sausage and grits, chocolate chip pancakes, juice and more. Michael eats about 3,000 calories just for breakfast! He swims about seven miles every day, so he needs a lot of food. His swimming partner, Cory Knopp, tries to eat more than Michael, but he can't. Michael always wins the eating contest.

Michael goes to school all day. In the afternoon, he swims for three more hours. He does not have a lot of free time. Sometimes he goes to a football or basketball game, but he usually goes to bed early. He swims almost 365 days a year. Michael likes to train hard, and he loves competition. He is still young, but he makes world records in 100 meter, 200 meter and 400 meter races. He has eight Olympic medals from the 2004 Summer Games. Six of the medals are gold. Michael is the fastest swimmer in the world. He's at home in the water. He's a human fish!

READING AND VOCABULARY SKILLS

A. Understanding the Main Ideas

1. Write T for true and F for false.

a. _____ Michael Phelps swims a lot.

b. _____ Michael Phelps does not eat a lot.

c. _____ Michael Phelps has Olympic gold medals.

d. _____ Michael Phelps makes world records.

e. _____ Michael's body is perfect for moving on land but not for swimming.

2. Put the sentences in the correct order.

    a. _____ Michael goes to school after breakfast.

    b. _____ Before school, he eats breakfast at his favorite restaurant.

    c. __1__ At 7:00, he starts swimming.

    d. _____ Michael stretches and does exercises after morning swim practice.

    e. _____ He goes to bed early.

    f. _____ In the afternoon he swims for three more hours.

B. Finding Details

Draw a line from the main idea to its details.

1. He swims a lot.

2. He eats a lot.

3. Michael's body is perfect for swimming.

He eats about 3,000 calories just for breakfast!

He has an extra long body and extra long arms. He has big feet, like the flippers of a fish.

He swims about 7 miles a day.

C. Learning New Words

Complete the sentences with words from the box.

wake up	calories	races	competitions
early	miles	exercises	go to bed

1. I _____ in the morning. I _____ at night.

2. *Late* is the opposite of _____.

3. Kilometers are like _____.

4. _____ make your body strong.

5. _____ and _____ are similar. They always have winners and losers.

6. Michael Phelps needs a lot of _____ because he exercises so much.

D. Using New Words

Ask a partner the questions.

1. What time do you *wake up* in the morning? What time do you *go to bed* at night?
2. Do you like to *wake up* early? Do you like to go to bed *early*?
3. Do you do *exercises*?
4. How many *miles* from school do you live?
5. Do you like *competitions*?
6. How many *calories* do most adults need every day?

E. Understanding Adverbs of Frequency

SKILL BUILDER

Adverbs of frequency tell us how often something happens. *Always, usually, never* and *sometimes* are some examples of these adverbs.

Work with a partner. Look at Michael's schedule. Write the correct adverb of frequency.

	eat breakfast	go to bed early	watch TV	run
Sunday	x	x	x	
Monday	x	x		
Tuesday	x	x		
Wednesday	x	x	x	
Thursday	x	x		
Friday	x		x	
Saturday	x			
How often?	*always*			

Look again at Michael's schedule. Write sentences about it using an adverb of frequency.

Example: *He always eats breakfast.*

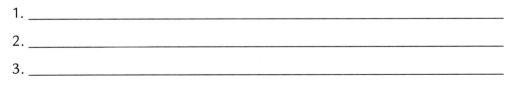

1. _____
2. _____
3. _____

F. Using *Before* and *After*

1. Circle the correct answer.

   a. Michael stretches <u>after</u> swimming.
      Which is first?   stretches   swimming

   b. Michael eats breakfast <u>before</u> school.
      Which is first?   breakfast   school

2. Look at the days of the week in Michael's schedule in Exercise E.
   Complete the sentences with *before* or *after*.

   a. Monday is _____ Tuesday.

   b. Thursday is _____ Wednesday.

   c. Friday is _____ Saturday.

   d. Sunday is _____ Saturday.

   e. Wednesday is _____ Thursday.

COMMUNICATING YOUR IDEAS

A. Talk About It

Talk about the questions with a small group.

1. Do you wake up early on the weekend?
2. Do you always eat breakfast? What do you eat?
3. Do you have a favorite restaurant? What is it? Why do you like it?
4. Do you exercise? Do you run, swim or ride a bicycle? Do you lift weights?
5. Do you have a lot of free time? What do you like to do in your free time?
6. Do you go to bed late on the weekend?

B. Draw It

Draw a chart of your weekly schedule. Share it with a partner.

C. Write About It

Write sentences about your schedule. Share some sentences with your class.

Examples: *I always drink coffee in the morning.*
               I wake up at six o'clock on Monday.

_____

_____

_____

EAT A RAINBOW

PRE-READING

1. Michael Phelps exercises a lot. He exercises more than most people.
   He also eats more than most people! Do you think he eats healthy food?
   Do you eat healthy food?

2. Work with a team. Write the names of foods that are the colors listed. The
   team with the most foods wins. You have 5 minutes!

Color	Foods
red	*tomatoes*
yellow	
orange	
green	
blue and purple	
white	

3. Write your list on the board. Are these foods good for you? Why or why not?

4. Look at the reading on the next page. Where is it from? What's the title?

Eat a Rainbow

Parents always ask, "How can I get my child to eat fruit and vegetables?" One answer is to teach your children to fill their bodies with color. Fruits and vegetables come in so many beautiful colors. Every different color is good for us.

Orange and yellow fruits and vegetables such as sweet potatoes and mangoes are healthy. They have many vitamins.

Orange

Dark green foods like spinach and broccoli are very healthy.

Green

Red foods like tomatoes and red peppers have Vitamin C.

Red

Blue or purple fruits and vegetables such as blueberries and red cabbage are also good for you.

Blue

What about the color white? White is not a color of the rainbow! White bread is not very healthy, but whole wheat bread is good for you. Too much sugar and salt are not good for you. Of course, some white foods, like yogurt, cottage cheese and tofu are very good for you.

Finally, remember the most important thing. Parents need to be good examples. You need to eat a rainbow, too!

READING AND WORD STUDY SKILLS

A. Understanding the Main Ideas

Circle the most important idea of the reading.

1. Red foods like tomatoes and red peppers have Vitamin C.

2. Eating fruits and vegetables of different colors is good for you.

3. Mangoes and blueberries are good for you.

B. Finding Details

Write T for true or F for false.

1. _____ Sweet potatoes and mangoes are good for you.

2. _____ Spinach and broccoli are healthy.

3. _____ Red foods have Vitamin B.

4. _____ No white food is good for you.

5. _____ Parents do not need to eat a rainbow.

C. Learning New Words

Draw a line to complete each sentence.

1. Thank you! The flowers are	a. <u>fill</u> my glass with water?
2. Would you please	b. <u>are good for you</u>.
3. Oranges	c. <u>healthy</u> food.
4. You can take	d. <u>beautiful</u>.
5. It's a good idea to eat	e. <u>Vitamin</u> C when you are sick.

D. Using New Words

Write sentences using the underlined words from exercise C.

1. _____

2. _____

3. _____

4. _____

5. _____

COMMUNICATING YOUR IDEAS

A. Talk About It

Talk with a small group.

1. Do you like to eat fruits and vegetables? What are your favorites?

2. What do you eat for breakfast? Lunch? Dinner?

3. What are some of your favorite dishes? Describe them.

4. Do you eat snacks? Explain.

5. Do you eat healthy food? Explain.

6. Do you and your family "eat a rainbow"?

B. Write About It

Write about what you like to eat.

Example: *I like to eat blueberries for breakfast.*
             I love roast beef with gravy and potatoes.

1. _____

2. _____

3. _____

4. _____

C. Draw It

Make a picture of fruits and vegetables of the rainbow. Draw, paint or use magazine pictures. Write the names of the foods. Share your poster with the class.

D. Role Play

Michael Phelps often goes to his favorite restaurant for breakfast. Do you like to eat in restaurants? Work with a small group. Practice a role play in a restaurant. Take the parts of a waitperson and customers. The expressions below will help you.

Waitperson	Customers
Would you like something to drink?	I would like_____
Are you ready to order?	Can I have more _____, please?
How is everything?	Excuse me, can we have the check, please?
Would you like some dessert or coffee?	
Can I get you anything else?	

Present your role play to the class.

■ **Internet or Library Research**

Find the Food Pyramid Guide on the Internet or in the library. Write about what you often eat in each category. Or find a website or magazine with photos of Michael Phelps and his Olympic swim team.

■ **Food Art**

Work with a group to make food art. Design your project. Use foods of many colors of the rainbow. Make your project and share it with the class. Vote on the best food art.

■ **Plan a Dinner Party**

Work with a group. Decide how many people you will invite to your dinner party. Make an invitation. Then plan a menu. Include foods of different colors. Make a list of what you need to buy.

■ **Guest Speaker**

Invite a nurse or nutritionist to come to your class. Write three questions about staying healthy. Ask him or her your questions.

■ **In Your Journal**

Write your daily schedule in your journal. Or write a list of everything you do to stay healthy for three days. Do you have healthy habits?

■ **CNN.**

Watch the CNN® video clip for this unit.

LEARNING TO LEARN

GETTING READY

1. Look at the picture. Who are the people? Where are they? What are they doing? Why are they happy?

2. Read the statements. Check (✓) Agree or Disagree. Discuss your answers in groups.

	Agree	Disagree
Learning English is easy.	☐	☐
Good students do not need to study.	☐	☐
It's important to do homework.	☐	☐
You must study all the time.	☐	☐
Organizing your time well helps you with school.	☐	☐

LITTLE STEPS, BIG STEPS

PRE-READING

Look at the pictures. Talk about what is happening in each picture. Then listen to your teacher read the story. Point to the correct picture.

LITTLE STEPS, BIG STEPS

Rene grew up in an Indian village in Oaxaca, Mexico. His family lived in a small house with a dirt floor. They spoke an Indian language. Rene started school in the village when he was six years old. There was no school for older children in the village. So Rene moved to Oaxaca City when he was nine years old. This was a big step for Rene. It was his first time in a city.

Little Rene got a job. He worked for a rich family. He took care of the house. He worked in the day, and he went to school at night. He learned good work habits and good study habits. He learned Spanish, and he grew up.

When Rene was thirteen years old, he returned to his village. He had many brothers and sisters. His mother needed help. Rene felt bad. He could not go to high school,

When Rene was twenty years old, he took a very big step. He went to Los Angeles. He worked as a cook and dishwasher. He took English classes. Then he went to a university. He studied very hard.

Today, Rene teaches English. He tells his students, "Learning English is not so hard. Having good habits is the important thing! Be organized. Use your time well. Have a good attitude."

READING AND WORD STUDY SKILLS

A. Understanding the Main Ideas

Rene took many big steps in his life. Complete the chart.

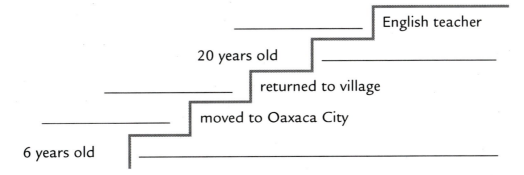

_____ English teacher

20 years old _____

_____ returned to village

_____ moved to Oaxaca City

6 years old _____

B. Finding Details

There is a mistake in each sentence. Correct it.

1. Rene spoke ~~Spanish~~ *an Indian language* when he was a little boy.

2. Rene got a job with a poor family.

3. He worked at the house during the night.

4. Rene has no brothers and sisters.

5. Today, Rene teaches Spanish.

C. Learning New Words

Complete these sentences from the story with the correct word from the box.

first	studied	moved	took care of
attitude	learned	step	rich

1. He _____ to Oaxaca City.

2. This was a big _____ for Rene.

3. It was his _____ time in a city.

4. He worked for a _____ family.

5. He _____ the house.

6. He _____ Spanish.

7. He _____ very hard.

8. He tells his students, " Have a good _____."

D. Using New Words

Complete the sentence with a word from exercise C.

1. The mother _____ her children.

2. Who was your _____ teacher?

3. The first _____ to learning a new language is to practice.

4. Carlos _____ to a new city.

5. I _____ how to walk when I was a baby.

6. Michele _____ hard for the test. She got a good grade.

7. His boss said, "You do good work. You have a good _____."

8. Mikako has a _____ father.

E. Verbs

Verbs are action words. *Run, talk* and *work* are verbs. Circle the verbs in the list.

walk   house   cat   sleep   school   drive   blue   eat   dance   swim

F. Simple Past Tense Verb Forms

SKILL BUILDER

There are regular and irregular simple past tense verb forms. Regular past tense verbs add –ed to the end of the verb. Some examples of regular past tense verbs are *cooked, listened* and *studied*. Irregular past tense verbs have many forms. Some examples of irregular verbs are *eat – ate, go – went, speak – spoke*.

Complete the chart. Write the verb. Check (✓) if the verbs are regular or irregular.

Verb — present	Verb — past	Regular	Irregular
live	lived	✓	
speak	spoke		✓
	started		
grow up			
	took		
	went		
want			
	was		

COMMUNICATING YOUR IDEAS

A. Talk About It

Discuss the questions with a small group. Use the verbs in past tense from your chart above when you need to. Then share your answers with the class.

1. Where did you grow up?

2. What is your native language?

3. When did you start studying English?

4. Why are you studying English?

5. What was your first job? What job do you want in the future?

6. What big steps did you take in your life?

B. Write About It

What steps do you want to take to learn English? Write three sentences below. Share them with your class.

Example: *I want to speak English with my neighbors.*

1. _____

2. _____

3. _____

C. Write About It

Look back at Rene's big steps on page 51. Draw big steps for your life.

DO YOU WANT BETTER GRADES?

PRE-READING

1. Look at Tanya and her friend. What is happening in the picture?

2. Read the questions below. Then ask a partner the questions. Report your answers back to the class.

	Me	My partner
Do you often talk to your friends and study at the same time?		
Do you usually watch TV and study at the same time?		
Do you usually stay up late to study for a test?		
Do you always do your homework?		

3. Tanya got a bad grade on her test. She read this flyer on her classroom bulletin board. She learned many things.

Do you want better grades?

The Tutorial Center helps students with their classes. Our tutors do individual and group tutoring. Tutors do not complete your homework for you, but they will help you learn how to do it. We also have Study Skills Workshops. Before you visit us, take a good look at the Study Tips below. These are the first steps to academic success at college!

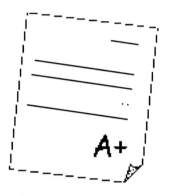

THE FIRST STEPS TO GETTING GOOD GRADES:

- ✓ Do your homework.
- ✓ Study in a quiet place.
- ✓ Take notes in class.
- ✓ Take short breaks.
- ✓ Join a study group with your classmates.
- ✓ Ask for help from your teacher.
- ✓ Have a positive attitude!

- ✗ Don't study when you are tired.
- ✗ Don't stay up late the night before a test.
- ✗ Don't listen to TV or listen to loud music while you study.
- ✗ Don't study on a bed or sofa.
- ✗ Don't talk to your friends when you study.

Come see us or look at our website for a schedule of workshops.

Tutorial Center Hours: Monday – Friday from 8:00 A.M. to 7:30 P.M.
Location: Library room L17
Contact: Catherine at 555–0011

READING AND WORD STUDY SKILLS

A. Understanding the Main Ideas

Circle the correct answer.

1. The Tutorial Center is a good place
   a. to get help with classes.   b. to meet new friends.

2. There are many things you can do
   a. to study English.   b. to get good grades.

B. Finding Details

Write yes or no.

1. _____ Do the tutors at the Tutorial Center do homework for students?

2. _____ Does the Tutorial Center have Study Skills Workshops?

3. _____ Is it a good idea to stay up late the night before a test?

4. _____ Is it a good idea to study on a bed ?

5. _____ Is it a good idea to take short breaks when you study?

Write the information.

6. When is the Tutorial Center open? _____

_____

7. Where is the Tutorial Center? _____

_____

8. What is the phone number of the Tutorial Center? _____

_____

9. Who can you contact for information? _____

_____

10. How does the Tutorial Center help students? Name two ways. _____

_____

_____

_____

C. Learning and Using New Words

| tutor | take notes | help |
| join | break | stay up |

Write each word from the box next to its definition. Then solve the puzzle.

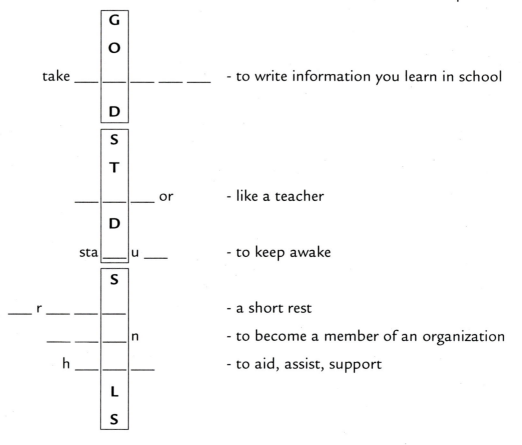

take ___ |G| ___ ___ ___   - to write information you learn in school
         |O|
         |D|

___ ___ |S| or   - like a teacher
         |T|
         |D|

sta ___ |u| ___   - to keep awake

___ r ___ ___ |S| - a short rest

___ ___ |S| n   - to become a member of an organization

h ___ |S| ___   - to aid, assist, support
      |L|
      |S|

COMMUNICATING YOUR IDEAS

A. Talk About It

Work with a small group. Look back at the picture on page 55. Tanya needs to learn good study skills. Tell Tanya what she should do.

Example: *Tanya should turn off the television.*
She shouldn't study late at night.

B. Interviewing

Interview a partner. Ask these questions. Write complete answers.

1. Where do you usually study? _____

_____

_____

2. When do you usually study? _____

_____

_____

3. Do you study alone or with a friend? _____

_____

_____

4. What is one of your good study habits? _____

_____

_____

5. What is one of your bad study habits? _____

_____

_____

ONE STEP BEYOND

■ **On the Internet**

Rene studied hard in school. He learned good study habits. Look on the Internet for study tips. Write three suggestions from the website.

■ **Video**

Watch a segment from *El Norte* and write about some of the steps in the characters' lives.

■ **Guest Speaker**

Invite a counselor from your school or community to talk with the class about good and bad study habits.

■ **Class Visit**

Go to the tutorial center at your school or a local college. Find out what kind of services they offer.

■ **In Your Journal**

Write about your study habits. What good study habits do you have? What bad study habits do you have? What should you do?

■ **CNN.**

Watch the CNN® video clip for this unit.

A FRIEND FOR LIFE

GETTING READY

1. Who are the people in the pictures? Where are they? What are they doing?

2. Do you have a good friend? What do you like to do together? Do you have friends who help you? How do they help you?

TOKYO'S FAMOUS DOG

PRE-READING

1. How do you get to work or school? Do you go by yourself or with other people?

2. Work with a partner. Write the word from the list under the correct picture.

professor	remember	wait	sick	statue
morning	take a train	evening	die	

morning

3. Read the words again. Look at the photo. Read the title of the story. What
   do you think happens in the story? Listen to your teacher read the story.

TOKYO'S FAMOUS DOG

Mr. Eisaburo Uyeno was a professor at the
Imperial University in Tokyo, Japan. He had a
special friend. The friend was a dog named
Hachiko. The dog's nickname was Hachi.

Every morning, the dog and Mr. Uyeno
walked together to the Shibuya Train
Station in Tokyo. The professor said
"goodbye" to Hachi and took the train to
work. Hachi waited for the professor at the
train station. Every evening the professor
returned from the university on the train.
Hachi was waiting for him.

One morning the professor and Hachi
walked to the train station as usual. The
professor said "goodbye" to Hachi and got
on the train. That day, the professor got
very sick at work, and he died. In the
evening, Hachi was waiting for the
professor at the train station. The professor
never returned on the train.

Every day Hachi continued to wait at
Shibuya Train Station for the professor. People at the train station saw Hachi every
day. They saw him every day for ten years! Sometimes they talked to Hachi or gave
him food. Finally, on March 8, 1935, Hachi died. Where did he die? He died at
Shibuya Train Station.

People thought Hachi was a very good friend to the professor. They wanted to
remember Hachi. They put a statue of Hachi at Shibuya Train Station.

Today, people still remember Hachi. The statue of Hachi is a popular meeting
place. Shibuya Train Station is very busy. If you want to meet a friend near Shibuya
Train Station, you can say, "Meet me at the Hachi."

A. Understanding the Main Ideas

Draw a line to connect the sentences.

1. The story is about   at the train station.

2. Every day Hachi waited for   a dog and a professor.
   the professor
                                          waiting for the
3. One day the professor   professor.

4. For ten years people saw Hachi   a statue of Hachi.

5. People made   today.

6. People still remember Hachi   died.

B. Finding Details

Circle the correct answer.

1. The professor worked at the _____.

   a. Hachiko University
   b. train station
   c. Imperial University

2. People at the train station _____.

   a. gave food to Hachi
   b. forgot Hachi
   c. took photos of Hachi

3. Hachi died _____.

   a. in 1953
   b. in 1935
   c. in 1835

4. Today, when people want to meet a friend near Shibuya Train Station,
   they say, _____.

   a. "See you later!"
   b. "Meet me at the Hachi!"
   c. "Call me at home!"

C. Learning New Words

Complete each sentence with the correct word from the box.

took the train	returned	died	nickname

1. A short name is a _____.

2. Last year I was very sad. My friend _____.

3. Mr. Uyeno _____ to work every day.

4. Last night my mother _____ from vacation.

evening	waited	statue	meet

5. The _____ of Liberty in New York City is very famous.

6. I like to _____ my friends after class.

7. Yesterday after class, I _____ for my friends in the cafeteria.

8. I eat dinner at 6:00 in the _____.

D. Using New Words

Find the words from exercise C in the word search.

D	S	R	J	H	A	V	M	E	E	T	H	F	A	D
P	E	T	Z	Z	J	A	F	C	X	C	Y	M	K	I
X	T	N	A	F	E	H	E	G	D	M	J	A	N	E
N	I	A	R	T	E	H	T	K	O	O	T	G	I	D
K	J	P	J	U	U	W	L	G	G	Z	N	W	C	E
E	N	X	D	A	W	E	X	I	Q	I	I	N	K	T
R	E	T	U	R	N	E	D	I	N	D	O	I	N	B
B	S	I	L	B	P	E	R	E	O	C	M	Q	A	D
W	A	I	T	E	D	K	V	P	R	D	L	T	M	T
T	O	O	K	T	H	E	T	R	A	I	N	A	E	E

E. Pronouns

Circle the correct meaning of the pronoun.

1. The professor took <u>it</u> to work.
   a. train   b. school

2. <u>They</u> made a statue.
   a. the professor   b. people

3. <u>He</u> waited for the professor.
   a. people   b. Hachi

4. The professor walked with <u>him</u>.
   a. the train   b. Hachi

F. Adjectives

Adjectives are words that describe nouns. (Remember: nouns are people, places and things.) *Blue*, *small*, *hot* and *delicious* are adjectives.

The car is <u>blue</u>.

I live in a <u>small</u> house.

It is <u>hot</u>.

These are <u>delicious</u> cookies.

Work with your partner. Do you know the meanings of the adjectives below? These adjectives describe people. Look back to page 61. Think about the people in the pictures. What words describe the friends in the pictures? Circle the words that describe a good friend.

nice	kind	caring	angry	happy
funny	generous	selfish	polite	helpful
other: _____		other: _____		

COMMUNICATING YOUR IDEAS

A. Talk About It

Discuss the questions below with a small group.

1. Do you have a pet? Describe it.

2. Do you have a nickname? If yes, what is it?

3. Do you walk to school or work? Do you take a train? Bus? Car? Bicycle?

4. What animal do people say is "man's best friend"? Why do people think so?

5. Do you have a special friend? Tell about him or her.

B. Write About It

Write about a pet you have or animal you like. Use the example below. Share with your class.

I have a bird. She is beautiful. Her name is Belle. She is a parrot. She is blue with white and black on her face. She has yellow on her wings.

_____

_____

_____

_____

_____

_____

A FRIEND IN NEED...

PRE-READING

1. Read the dictionary entry for "proverb." What is the definition of "proverb"? Discuss the questions with your partner.

> **proverb** /ˈprɑvərb/ *n.* a short saying rich in meaning: *"Man's best friend is his dog"* is a proverb.

    a. Do dogs make good friends?

    b. What are the special qualities of dogs?

2. Work in a group. Read the proverbs about friends below.

    a. Where is each proverb from?

    b. Do you know what each proverb means?

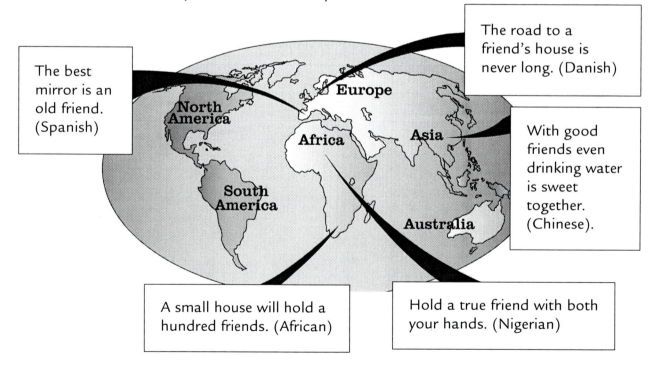

The road to a friend's house is never long. (Danish)

The best mirror is an old friend. (Spanish)

With good friends even drinking water is sweet together. (Chinese).

A small house will hold a hundred friends. (African)

Hold a true friend with both your hands. (Nigerian)

LAST LESSON FOR THE GRADUATES

Graduation is coming! Many students are leaving the college. What are they taking with them? A lot of things for sure, but the most important thing is friends.

We asked some teachers to give us one last lesson. The lesson is proverbs about friends. Proverbs teach people about life. Older people often teach proverbs to younger people. Every culture has proverbs. They are short and easy to remember.

Dr. Schmidt says, "I have a favorite proverb about friends. 'Friendship is a plant we must water.' It is German. It means that we need to take care of friends like we take care of a garden."

Mrs. Minelli says, "Only your real friends will tell you when your face is dirty" is a Sicilian proverb. This is important to remember. It means that only good friends tell you when you are making a mistake."

Dr. Tulga says "My grandfather in Turkey told me, 'Nobody is so rich that he can throw away a friend.' It means that everyone needs friends. Be good to them."

The good news is: there is no test for this lesson. The bad news is: we will miss you.

Goodbye, friends! Don't forget us!

READING AND WORD STUDY SKILLS

A. Understanding the Main Ideas

Circle T for true or F for false.

1. The teachers have a last lesson for graduating students.   T   F

2. A proverb teaches a lesson.   T   F

3. A proverb is a not easy to remember.   T   F

4. Older people often teach proverbs to younger people.   T   F

B. Finding Details

Draw a line from the proverb to its meaning.

1. Nobody is so rich that he can throw away a friend.   Take care of friends like we take care of a garden.

2. Only your real friends will tell you when your face is dirty.   Everyone needs friends.

Good friends tell you when you are making a mistake.

3. Friendship is a plant we must water.

C. Learning New Words

Unscramble the words from the article. Then draw a line from the word to its definition.

1. getorf   f __ __ __ __ __   a. not clean

2. gradne   __ __ r __ __ __   b. to not remember

3. tydri   __ __ r __ __   c. a place where plants grow

4. aeiofvrt   __ __ __ __ __ __ __ e   d. do this with garbage

5. wohtr aawy __ __ __ __ w __ w __ __   e. I really like it

D. Using New Words

Complete the sentences with the words from Exercise C.

1. My _____ singer is playing in a concert on Saturday.

2. The little boy washed his hands. They were _____.

3. Remember and _____ are opposites.

4. My grandmother likes to plant tomatoes in her _____.

5. Restaurants _____ a lot of food in the United States.

COMMUNICATING YOUR IDEAS

A. Talk About It

Ask your partner the questions.

1. Do you know a very kind person? Explain.

2. Do you have a funny friend? Explain.

3. Do you know a selfish person? Explain.

4. Do you know a very generous person? Explain.

B. Draw It

Draw a picture of one of the proverbs from Part 2. Show the picture to your classmates. Let them guess which proverb your picture shows.

C. Write About It

Write sentences about what makes a good friend. Use the adjectives you learned in this unit. Share them with your class.

Example: *A good friend is kind.*

_____

_____

_____

_____

■ **Internet**

Find songs about friendship in English on the Internet. Write the titles. Share them with your class.

■ **Interview an English Speaker**

There is a traditional song about friends. It is also a proverb. The words are "Make new friends but keep the old, one is silver and the other's gold." Ask an English speaker about it. Ask what the proverb means. Ask the person to teach the song to you. Then teach the song to your class!

■ **Movie**

Watch *Milo and Otis* or *Turner and Hooch*. In your journal, write three ways the friends helped each other.

■ **More Reading**

Read the children's book *The Giving Tree* by Shel Silverstein or *The Rainbow Fish* by Marcus Pfister. Who are the friends in the story? Describe them.

■ **Music**

Listen to *You've Got a Friend* or another song about friends. What is one message the singer is giving the friend?

■ **Collage**

Make a collage of pictures of things you like to do with your friends and family. Show it to the class.

■ **In Your Journal**

Write about a special friend. Use some of the vocabulary words you learned in this unit.

■ **CNN.**®

Watch the CNN® video clip for this unit.

SURVIVAL

GETTING READY

Look at the photos. Work with a partner. Write the number of the photo next to the sport activity below. Ask, "Would you do these sports? Why or why not?"

___kayaking   ___bungee jumping   ___rock climbing   ___parachuting

1. Now count your classmates. How many people would do 1?_____
   2?_____ 3?_____ 4?_____

2. Which sport is the least popular? Why ?

THE LONG RESCUE

PRE-READING

Look at the pictures. Look at the title. What is a rescue? What do you think will happen next in the story? Listen to your teacher read the story.

crevasse

THE LONG RESCUE

Geoff loves to hike and climb. In May 2004, he went to Oregon to climb to the top of Mt. Hood. He went with his best friend, Marc. They were at 9,400 feet. It was snowy and cold. Suddenly, Geoff fell into a hole called a crevasse. His body hit the sides of the crevasse like a pinball in a pinball machine. Marc called, "Geoff? Geoff?" but there was no answer. He could not see Geoff. Marc was worried. Was Geoff dead?

Marc quickly went down the mountain to get help. Marc saw three men below. They had a cell phone. They called 911. Then the three men went back up the mountain with Marc. They looked into the crevasse and called Geoff's name. This time Geoff answered. They knew he was alive. One man named Mike went 65 feet down on a rope. He found Geoff at the bottom.

Geoff could not move his legs. He had cuts. His eye was hurt. He had broken bones. He was in pain, but he was happy to see Mike. Mike put a sleeping bag around him to keep him warm. Two hours later the Portland Mountain Rescue team arrived. They went into the crevasse to bring Geoff up in a special rescue basket. It was a dangerous and difficult rescue.

Finally, ten hours after he fell, Geoff was safe in a hospital. He was there for three weeks. He had many injuries. Geoff was very lucky to be alive. Marc visited him every day. Geoff said, "I want to come back to Oregon next May. I still want to climb Mt. Hood." Marc said, "OK. I want to go with you, and the rescue team does, too!"

READING AND WORD STUDY SKILLS

A. Understanding the Main Ideas

Put the sentences in the correct order.

_____ Geoff and Marc went to climb Mt. Hood.

_____ Geoff still wants to climb Mt. Hood.

_____ Geoff fell into a crevasse.

___1___ Geoff loves to hike and climb.

_____ Geoff was hurt.

_____ The rescue team went down to bring Geoff up.

B. Finding Details

1. Circle the correct words.

   a. Mt. Hood is in _____.
   California   Oregon   Washington

   b. Marc is Geoff's _____.
   brother   doctor   best friend

   c. Geoff could not move _____.
   arms   legs   head

   d. The rescue took _____.
   a few minutes   a few days   many hours

2. Draw a line to complete each sentence from the story.

   a. Marc quickly went down the mountain   to keep him warm.

                                      to get help.

   b. The rescue team had a special basket   to bring Geoff up.

   c. Mike went down 65 feet   to find Geoff.

   d. He put a sleeping bag around Geoff

C. Learning New Words

Circle the correct word.

1. Geoff loves to _____.
   a. climb   b. walk

2. Geoff _____ into a deep hole.
   a. jumped   b. fell

3. When they called Geoff's name, he _____.
   a. smiled   b. answered

4. Mike went down into the _____ to find Geoff.
   a. hole   b. house

5. The men from the _____ team arrived to bring Geoff up.
   a. rescue   b. soccer

6. Geoff was _____.
   a. sad   b. hurt

7. He had _____ bones.
   a. good   b. broken

8. Geoff was alive. He was _____.
   a. lucky   b. young

D. Using New Words

Complete each sentence with the correct word.

climb	answered	fell	lucky

1. Tony is _____ because he has a nice family.

2. I _____ the telephone when it rang.

3. My brother likes to _____ mountains.

4. When baby Brian tried to walk, he sometimes _____.

broken	hole	hurt	rescue

5. There is a _____ in my shoe.

6. Luis has a _____ arm.

7. The _____ team helps people.

8. I sometimes _____ my back when I play tennis.

E. Antonyms

Write the antonyms from the story.

1. dead   a __ __ __ __

2. bottom   __ __ p

3. up   __ __ w __

4. dangerous   __ __ __ e

F. Using your Dictionary

Dictionaries can tell you what <u>part of speech</u> a word is. Example of parts of speech are nouns, verbs, and adjectives. Read the dictionary entry. What part of speech is the word *accident*? What is the definition? What is the example sentence?

---

accident /ˈæksədənt/ *noun*
something harmful or unpleasant that happens by surprise: *He had an accident on the way to work; he fell and broke an ankle.*

Now use the word in your own sentence.

_____

_____

What part of speech is the word *first aid*? What is the definition? What is the example sentence?

---

first aid *noun*
emergency medical treatment given before the injured person receives whatever further treatment may be necessary: *When the worker received a bad cut on his hand, a co-worker administered first aid and then took him to the hospital.*

Now use the word in your own sentence.

_____

_____

COMMUNICATING YOUR IDEAS

A. Talk About It

Ask a partner the questions.

1. Do you climb mountains?

2. What activity do you love to do?

3. Do you have a best friend? Who is it?

4. What do you like to do with your best friend?

5. Do you have a rescue story? Tell it.

6. What do you do when you are hurt?

B. Role-playing

1. Look at the picture. Write the number next to the body part.

   _____ Eye   _____ Arm

   _____ Ear   _____ Shoulder

   _____ Knee   _____ Nose

   _____ Stomach   _____ Hand

   _____ Back   _____ Leg

   _____ Neck   _____ Foot

2. Work with a partner. Practice the conversation below.

   A: *"I don't feel well."*

   B: *"What's wrong?"*

   A: *"My stomach hurts."*

   B: *"You should see a doctor."*

SURVIVAL TIPS

1. Do you know what to do if someone has an accident? How can you learn about what to do when someone has an accident?

2. Look at the leaflet below. It is from a first aid class. Look at the pictures. Work in groups. Discuss what is happening.

What to do in case of an accident:

1. Don't panic. Check for danger. Are you or the accident victim in danger?

2. Stay calm. Check the victim's pulse and breathing if he cannot answer you.

3. Call 911 or the emergency operator. Tell the operator what happened and where you are.

4. Don't leave the victim alone. Wait for help if possible.

5. Keep the victim safe and warm. Put a blanket on him. Don't move the victim unless necessary. Wait for medical help.

6. Talk to the victim. Ask the victim if he is okay. Tell him that help is on the way.

7. Keep a positive attitude.

READING AND WORD STUDY SKILLS

A. Understanding the Main Ideas

Circle the correct answer.

1. This is a leaflet for _____.
   a. an English class   b. a first aid class

2. The leaflet tells things to do and not do in case of an _____.
   a. accident   b. fire

B. Finding Details

Write T for true or F for false.

_____ 1. Stay calm.

_____ 2. Call your friend to report the accident.

_____ 3. Don't talk to the victim.

_____ 4. Keep the victim cool.

_____ 5. Don't leave the victim alone.

C. Learning New Words

Look at the underlined word. Draw a line from the word to its definition.

1. Ask the <u>victim</u> if he is okay.   a. be afraid and nervous

2. Don't <u>panic</u>.   b. good

3. Keep a <u>positive</u> attitude.   c. person who has accident,
                                                  sickness,etc.

D. Using New Words

Write your own sentences about Geoff and Marc using each of the underlined words from exercise C.

1. _____

2. _____

3. _____

E. Imperatives

We use the *imperative* to give orders and instructions.

Affirmative	Negative
Close your book.	Don't talk.
Spell your name.	Don't move.

Look back at the list of things to do in case of an accident on page 78. Complete the chart below.

Do these things	Don't do these things
Stay calm	**Don't panic**

COMMUNICATING YOUR IDEAS

A. Talk About It

Discuss these questions with a small group.

1. Did you ever see an accident? What happened?

2. What can you do to help in an accident?

3. Do you have a first aid kit at home? What is in it?

4. Can you call 911 or an emergency operator in your native country?

5. Where can you learn more about what to do in case of an accident?

B. Write About It

Write your own story about an accident or problem.

Example: *I was at the beach. I went swimming in the ocean. I was swimming when I felt something hit my face. It was a jellyfish. It hurt. The lifeguard put some special cream on my face. It made me feel better. I did not go back into the water.*

_____

_____

_____

C. Role Play

1. Brainstorm *accidents* with your teacher and class. Write them on the word web below.

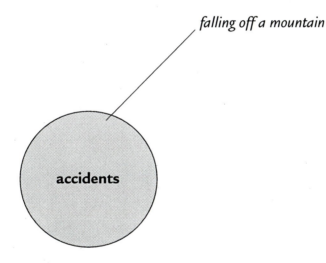

falling off a mountain

accidents

2. Work with a partner. Choose one situation from your word web. Write a short dialog to present to the class. Call 911 or the emergency operator to report an accident. One student is the operator, the other student is reporting the accident.

■ **Internet or Library Research**

Find out how search and rescue dogs helped at the World Trade Center.

Visit the Portland Mountain Rescue website. Find out how many rescues they make each year.

■ **Poster Project**

Get information from the Red Cross about making an emergency plan for your class or family. Tell people what they need to do or not do. Post it in your class or house.

■ **Movies**

Watch the movie *Touching the Void*. Describe the accident in your journal.

■ **Interview**

Invite volunteers from a local rescue group or the Red Cross to come to class. Prepare questions to ask them. Find out how you can be a volunteer.

■ **In Your Community**

Take a first aid or CPR course. Then volunteer with a local rescue group.

■ **CNN.**

Watch the CNN® video clip for this unit.

TRAVELING ACROSS AMERICA

GETTING READY

1. Look at the photo. Can you find a car? A taxi? A bus? A bicycle?

2. Work with a partner. Ask the questions below. Complete the chart.

	Me	My Partner
How do you usually go to school?		
How do you usually go to work?		
How do you usually travel around your country?		
How do you usually travel to other countries?		

PART ONE · MILES FOR MONEY

PRE-READING

1. Work with a partner. Look at the map of the United States. Match the number of the state with its name. Use a U.S. map to help you.

<u>1</u> Oregon

____ Vermont

____ New York

____ Minnesota

____ Wyoming

<u>10</u> New Hampshire

____ Michigan

____ Idaho

____ South Dakota

____ Wisconsin

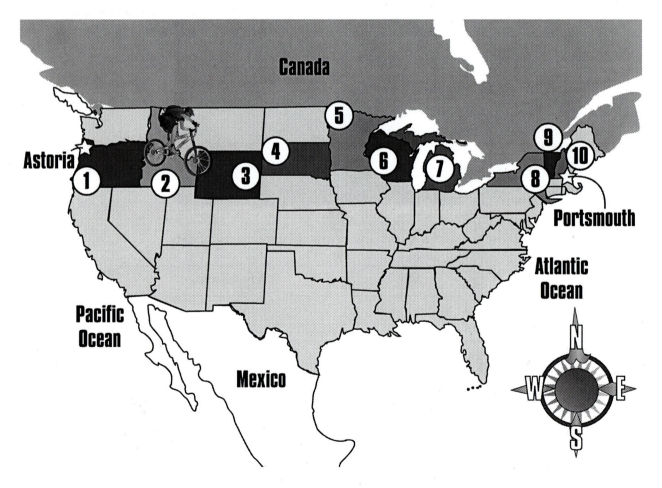

2. Work with a partner. Answer the questions.

    a. What ocean is the city of Astoria on?
    b. What ocean is the city of Portsmouth on?
    c. Which states are west of Wyoming?
    d. Which states are east of New York?
    e. What country is north of the U.S.?
    f. What country is south of the U.S.?

3. How many miles do you think it is from New Hampshire to Oregon? Listen to your teacher read the story and find out.

MILES FOR MONEY

Patricia Starr is a concert pianist and music teacher. She wanted to raise money for music scholarships at her local community college in California. One day she had an idea. She thought, "I'm going to ride my bicycle across the United States this summer. I'm going to ask people to give money for every mile I ride." She talked to people in her community about her idea. They liked it. People said, "I will give you money for every mile you ride." She was excited.

Patricia joined about fifty other bicycle riders. They began the 3,622-mile trip across the U.S. in Astoria, Oregon. Patricia rode through Oregon to Idaho and then onto Wyoming. Patricia went up and down huge hills. It was difficult. She continued through South Dakota, Minnesota and Wisconsin. She saw beautiful countryside. She met friendly people. But there were problems, too. The weather was sometimes very hot, windy or cold. Patricia was tired and sore every night.

She rode through Michigan, New York and Vermont. She went through Ontario, Canada, too. One day she had an accident. She fell off her bike and had bruises. But she continued to ride. She finished her bike ride fifty days later in Portsmouth, New Hampshire. She raised more than $10,000 for music scholarships. Patricia was happy and proud. She did it!

People don't believe her when she tells them her age. Patricia looks very young and acts very young. Can you believe that she is 67 years old? The 67-year-old went across the U.S. by bicycle in 50 days!

READING AND WORD STUDY SKILLS

A. Understanding the Main Ideas

Circle the correct answer.

1. Patricia rode her bicycle across the United States
   a. to get exercise.   b. to raise money.

2. The bicycle trip was
   a. easy.   b. difficult.

3. At the end of the trip, Patricia was
   a. tired and sick.   b. happy and proud.

4. People can't believe that Patricia is
   a. a concert pianist.   b. 67 years old.

B. Finding Details

There is a mistake in each sentence. Find it and write the correct word(s) above.

1. Patricia is a concert ~~violinist~~ *pianist*.

2. She thought, "I'm going to ride my bicycle across the United States this winter."

3. She began the ride in Ashland, Oregon.

4. She rode her bicycle across twenty states.

5. She fell off her bike and had broken bones.

6. She raised more than $10,000 for English scholarships.

7. People don't believe that she is 32 years old.

C. Learning New Words

Look at the underlined word. Circle the correct meaning of the word.

1. Patricia wanted to <u>raise</u> more money.
   a. get   b. spend

2. People in her <u>community</u> wanted to help her.
   a. state   b. area where you live

3. She was <u>excited</u>.
   a. happy   b. tired

4. Patricia <u>rode</u> her bicycle across the U.S.
   a. sat on it and pedaled   b. sat on it

5. She <u>thought</u>, "I'm going to ride my bicycle across the U.S."
   a. wrote   b. said to herself

6. Patricia was tired and <u>sore</u> every night.
   a. she had pain   b. she was angry

7. She fell off her bike and had <u>bruises</u>.
   a. headaches
   b. black and blue marks on her skin

8. Patricia was happy and <u>proud</u>.
   a. pleased   b. shy

D. Using New Words

Complete the sentences with the correct word.

raise	excited	community	rode

1. We need to _____ money to build a new church.

2. I _____ my bike to the park.

3. The people in my _____ are very friendly.

4. The children were _____ about the trip.

bruises	sore	proud	thought

5. My sister is _____ because she passed her driver's license test.

6. I have _____ feet from walking a lot.

7. Eric was in an accident. He has some _____.

8. We _____ about the problem.

E. Using *going to*

We can express the future with *be + going to + verb*.

Examples: *I **am going to take** a trip next week.*
*My brother **is going to buy** some new music CDs.*

Write 3 things that you are going to do this month.

_____

_____

_____

COMMUNICATING YOUR IDEAS

A. Talk About It

Discuss these questions with a small group.

1. Do you have a bicycle?

2. Where do you like to ride your bike?

3. Did you ever take a long bicycle trip? If yes, where did you go?

4. Would you like to bicycle across the U.S.? Why or why not?

5. Did you ever raise or give money to help other people? Explain.

B. Role Playing

1. Work in a small group. Write three questions to ask Patricia.

Example: *Where did you sleep at night?*

_____

_____

_____

2. Work with a partner. One student is the interviewer and the other student is Patricia. The interviewer can use the questions from above. Present your interview to the class.

PLANNING A VACATION

PRE-READING

Look at the name of the website. Look at the photos. Check (✓) the kinds of tours you can take.

_____ Bicycling   _____ Canoeing   _____ Sailing

_____ Walking   _____ Motor coach   _____ Cross-Country Skiing

_____ Hiking   _____ Horseback Riding

Address: http://www.backtonaturetours.net

Back to Nature Tours

Travel the beautiful United States with us. Enjoy the great outdoors for a wonderful adventure you will never forget.

Walk along the beautiful Blue Ridge Mountains. We will climb to the top of Grandfather Mountain and enjoy a picnic lunch. Three-day package available. Only $209. Includes all meals and lodging.

Ride horseback through the magnificent Grand Canyon. This trip lets you enjoy some of the most scenic views on earth. You can relax and go for a swim in the beautiful waterfalls at the bottom of the canyon. Seven-day package available. Only $495. Includes all meals, lodging and guide.

Bicycle along the peaceful roads of Vermont. We will ride through small towns and visit interesting places. At night, you can enjoy delicious dinners in our lovely bed and breakfast inns. Fourteen-day package available. Only $545. Includes lodging and guide.

For more information on our tours, click on the links on the right.

Walking Tours

Hiking Tours

Bicycling Tours

Horseback Riding Tours

Canoeing Tours

READING AND WORD STUDY SKILLS

A. Understanding the Main Ideas

Circle the correct answer.

1. This is a _website / magazine article_.

2. The tours go to _cities / natural places_.

3. These tours are for people who like _to be active / to sit._

4. The tours are _the same / different_.

B. Finding Details

1. Draw a line matching the activity with the place

   a. walk   in the beautiful waterfalls

   b. bicycle   along the beautiful Blue Ridge Mountains

   c. ride horseback   on top of Grandfather Mountain

   d. swim   through the magnificent Grand Canyon

   e. picnic   along the peaceful roads of Vermont

2. Look at the Back to Nature Tours website. Complete the chart below. Which tour would you choose? Explain.

Type of Tour?	Where?	How long?	How much?
Hiking Tour	Blue Ridge Mountains		
		7-day package	
	Vermont		$545

C. Learning New Words

Match the word with its definition. Write the letter.

_____ 1. outdoors   a. take it easy

_____ 2. peaceful   b. travel with a group

_____ 3. adventure   c. outside

_____ 4. tours   d. quiet and relaxing

_____ 5. relax   e. exciting experience

D. Using New Words

Complete each sentence with the correct word.

outdoors	peaceful	adventure	tours	relax

1. We like to eat _____ in the summer.

2. My friends Martin and Janet like to travel on _____.

3. It is _____ at night, but it is noisy in the daytime.

4. It is exciting to have a new _____.

5. I'm tired. I want to _____.

E. Using a Dictionary

Look at the dictionary entry for the word *guide*. What parts of speech is it? What are the definitions? What are the example sentences?

> **guide** /gaɪd/ *noun* a person who shows the way and often gives information, esp. to tourists: *A tour guide gave some history as we passed each important building.*
> **guide** *verb* **guided, guiding, guides** to show the way, give information: *A professor guided us through the museum.*

Now use the word in your own sentence.

_____

F. Prepositions

1. We use *prepositions* of place to describe where something is. Some examples are *in, on, next to, by* and *near*.

2. Look at the map. Use the words in the box to complete the sentences below.

next to	across from	between	on the corner

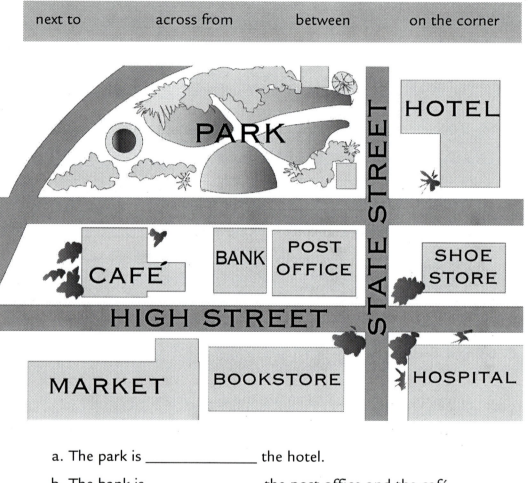

a. The park is _____ the hotel.

b. The bank is _____ the post office and the café.

c. The market is _____ the bookstore.

d. The park is _____.

3. Work with a partner. Look at the map. Practice asking and giving directions.

Example: *"Excuse me. Where is the post office?"*
             "It's next to the bank."

COMMUNICATING YOUR IDEAS

A. Talk About It

Discuss these questions in a small group.

1. Do you like the outdoors?
2. What kind of outdoor activities do you like to do?
3. Would you like to take an adventure tour? Why or why not?
4. How do you like to travel?
5. What places would you like to visit in the U.S.?

B. Vacation Activities

Brainstorm with your class about vacation activities.

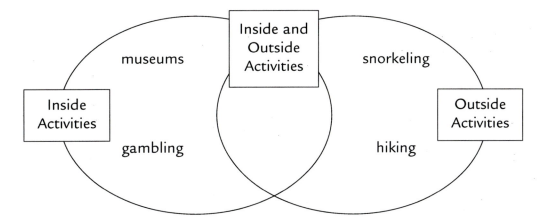

C. Planning a Trip

Congratulations! You have won a free trip to anywhere in the United States. Work with a small group. Decide where you want to go and answer the following questions. Use *be going to*. Then tell the class.

1. Where are you going to go?
2. When are you going to leave?
3. How are you going to travel?
4. What are you going to see?
5. What are you going to do?
6. When are you going to return?

ONE STEP BEYOND

■ **Internet**
Use the Internet to find information about traveling to different places. Choose a place you would like to visit and find out about it. How can you get there? What can you see? What can you do? Tell the class.

■ **Guest Speakers**
Invite someone from The Sierra Club or an adventure travel company to come to your class to talk about outdoor travel. Write questions to ask them.

■ **In the Community**
Go to your local Chamber of Commerce or Visitor's Information Center. Find information about interesting places you can visit in your area. Get maps of your area. Plan a field trip with your class.

■ **Movies**
Watch the movie *The Incredible Journey*. Where did they travel? What did they see?

■ **Songs**
Listen to the songs *This Land is Your Land* by Woody Guthrie, *Rocky Mountain High* and *Take Me Home, Country Roads* by John Denver. What places do the songs describe?

■ **In Your Journal**
Write about a trip you took or a trip you would like to take.

■ **CNN.**
Watch the CNN® video clip for this unit.

FASHION FEVER

GETTING READY

1. Look up the word *fashionable* in your dictionary. Are the people and clothes in the photos fashionable? Why?

2. Check (✓) the box to complete the chart.

HOW MUCH DO YOU LIKE FASHION?

How often do you...?	every day	once a week	once a month	every few months	never
...buy new clothes	☐	☐	☐	☐	☐
...get a haircut	☐	☐	☐	☐	☐
...read fashion magazines	☐	☐	☐	☐	☐
...watch TV shows about fashion	☐	☐	☐	☐	☐
...spend 30 or more minutes getting dressed	☐	☐	☐	☐	☐
...buy accessories (for example: earrings, necklaces)	☐	☐	☐	☐	☐
...use beauty products (for example: make-up, skin care, cologne, hair gel)	☐	☐	☐	☐	☐

Are you a fashion victim?
Mostly "every day" and "once a week" = You love fashion! You probably spend too much money on it.
Mostly "once a month" = You like fashion very much.
Mostly "every few months" = Fashion is a necessary evil for you. You only do it because you have to.
Mostly "never" = You have little interest in fashion.

3. Interview a partner. Ask the questions above.

Example: *"How often do you shop for clothes?" "Once a month."*

BLUE GOLD: LEVI STRAUSS

PRE-READING

Are you wearing jeans today? How many people in your class are wearing jeans today? What do jeans look like? Are jeans fashionable? Do you like wearing jeans?

Look at the pictures. Listen to your teacher tell the story.

BLUE GOLD: LEVI STRAUSS

Levi Strauss immigrated to the United States from Germany in 1847. His brothers were salesmen in New York. Levi started working with them, and he learned English.

Then Levi heard some exciting news. People were finding gold in California. Levi wanted to go to California, but he didn't want to look for gold. He wanted to be a salesman. Many people were moving to California. So, in 1853, Levi's brothers gave Levi blankets, tents, and clothes to sell in California.

Levi took a ship to San Francisco, but he sold everything on the ship! When he arrived, he only had material to make tents. In San Francisco, Levi tried to sell the material, but one miner said to Levi, "I don't need a tent. I need pants!" Miners always needed new pants. They needed very strong pants. So Levi sewed pants from the tent material to sell to miners.

Miners liked Levi's new pants. He sold a lot of them. In 1860, Levi's brothers sent a new material to him from New York. It was denim. It was more comfortable than tent material. Levi started making blue denim jeans, but there was one problem. Miners often ripped their jeans, so Levi and a partner put metal rivets in the jeans. The jeans were very strong this way, and they were a good price. They only cost 22 cents. In 1873, Levi and his family opened a factory in San Francisco.

Levi Strauss became a rich man. He was kind to his workers. He asked his workers to call him "Levi," not "Mr. Strauss." Levi liked to work. He said, "Money does not make me happy. Routine work makes me happy." He was generous. He gave his money to several organizations. For example, he gave money for twenty-eight scholarships at the University of California, Berkeley. He left the rest of his money and the company to his family. Levi Strauss died in San Francisco in 1902.

READING AND WORD STUDY SKILLS

A. Understanding the Main Ideas

Put the sentences in the correct order.

1. _____ Levi moved to California.

2. _____ Levi Strauss immigrated to the United States from Germany.

3. _____ He sold pants made from tent material.

4. _____ He made blue denim pants. He called them "jeans."

5. _____ Levi and his family opened a factory.

6. _____ They put metal rivets in the jeans.

B. Finding Details

1. Circle the correct answer.

    a. Levi's brothers were _____.
       miners   salesmen   teachers

    b. Miners always needed new _____.
       pants   tents   horses

    c. The jeans cost _____.
       12 dollars   22 dollars   22 cents

    d. Levi Strauss said, "_____ does not make me happy."
       jeans   money   love

2. Draw a line to complete the sentences.

a. Levi wanted to go to California,	but he sold everything on the ship!
b. Levi took a ship to San Francisco,	but one miner said to Levi, "I don't need a tent. I need pants!"
c. In San Francisco, Levi tried to sell the material,	but he didn't want to look for gold.

C. Learning and Using New Words

Complete each sentence with the correct word. Then write the word in the puzzle.

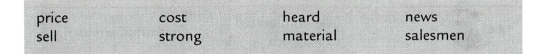

price	cost	heard	news
sell	strong	material	salesmen

Across

3. He is a _____ man. He can carry heavy things.
5. My pants are a soft, comfortable _____.
6. How much did your new computer _____?
7. I want to _____ my car for $8000.

Down

1. This morning I _____ the birds singing.
2. They changed the _____ because there is a sale.
3. My brothers are good _____. They can sell anything.
4. Did you hear the good _____? I won the lottery!

D. Using *When, What* and *Where*

Look back at the story. Complete the chart.

When?	What?	Where?
1847	Levi immigrated to America	from Germany
	Levi took a ship	to San Francisco
	Levi's brothers sent denim	
1873		in San Francisco
	Levi Strauss died	

Write sentences using the information from the chart.

Example: *In 1847 Levi came to America from Germany.*

1. _____

2. _____

3. _____

4. _____

COMMUNICATING YOUR IDEAS

A. Talk About It

Talk about the questions with your group.

1. Do you like to go shopping? How often do you go shopping? Where do you like to go shopping? Why?
2. Do you shop for things on sale? What do you buy?
3. Do you like to sew? If yes, what do you make?
4. Do you like to get dressed up for parties and weddings? How often do you get dressed up?

B. Doing A Survey

With your teacher, ask students the questions below. Write down how many students say *yes*. Then make a bar graph with your class.

1. Are you wearing jeans today? _____

2. Do you have five or more pairs of jeans? _____

3. Do you wear jeans four days a week or more? _____

4. Do you have a jean jacket? _____

5. Do you have jeans that are different colors (e.g., black, pink, white)? _____

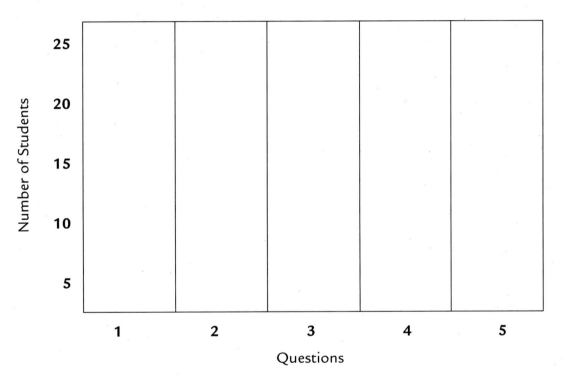

FASHION IN HARAJUKU

PRE-READING

1. Maja is visiting Japan with her Japanese friend Tomoko. Look at the photos she emailed to her friend Suzanne. What did she do? What did she see?

2. Read the e-mail. Put a check (✓) next to the sentences that are true.

    a. _____ Harajuku is a fashion district in Tokyo.

    b. _____ It is not very crowded on weekends.

    c. _____ Teenagers dress up in Harajuku.

    d. _____ There are no restaurants or shops in Harajuku.

```
To:      suz@coollink.net
Subject: Fashion in Harajuku
Send | Save | Print | Forward          ≡   ≡   ≡   B I U   ≡
```

Hi Suzanne,

I'm having a great time in Japan with Tomoko. Last Sunday, we went to Harajuku. It is a fun and crazy part of Tokyo. It is a fashion district. On the weekends, it is crowded! Lots of young people go to Harajuku.

There are lots of great restaurants and clothes shops in Harajuku. First we ate some delicious sushi, and then we shopped. The shops sell cool things that Japanese teenagers like. (I bought something special for you there!;-) Some famous fashion designers have offices here. They want to see the styles young people are wearing.

You would love Harajuku. The teenagers are so fashionable. Some people look like they are dressed up for Halloween. We saw two girls dressed in pink pajamas like babies! One girl was wearing a bright blue kimono, blue and white feathers in her hair and white makeup! She was wearing big, black boots with high heels. Those shoes didn't look very comfortable!

Wish you were here!

Maja

READING AND WORD STUDY SKILLS

A. Understanding the Main Ideas

Circle other possible titles for the e-mail.

Blue Kimono   Fun in Harajuku   Fashion

B. Finding Details

Circle the correct word to complete each sentence.

1. Maja is visiting Japan with _a tour group/Tomoko_.

2. Some famous _actors/fashion designers_ have offices in Harajuku.

3. Maja saw a girl wearing _pink/blue and white_ feathers in her hair.

4. Her big black boots _did not look/looked_ comfortable.

C. Learning New Words

Unscramble the words. Then draw a line from each word to its definition.

1. sspoh _____
2. credowd _____
3. albeshoinaf _____
4. pu sreds _____
5. ytsles _____

a. full of people
b. to get dressed in formal
   clothes or a costume
c. stores
d. popular at that time
e. ways of dressing

D. Drawing Conclusions

Write T for true and F for false.

1. _____ Suzanne likes fashion.
2. _____ Maja likes sushi.
3. _____ Maja wants to buy big, black boots with high heels.
4. _____ Maja is going to give a gift from Harajuku to Suzanne.

E. Word Groups

A good way to remember new words is to put them into groups. A common way to group words is by topic or theme. Putting words into groups can help you see how words are related to each other.

1. Look at the picture on page 107. Write the number next to the clothes words in the box.

___sandals	___t-shirt	___suit	___boots	___tennis shoes
___blouse	___shirt	___skirt	___jacket	
___purse	___pants	___tie	___belt	

2. Write the words from the box in the correct group. Some words may go in more than one group.

Women's clothes	Men's clothes	Footwear	Accessories

COMMUNICATING YOUR IDEAS

A. Talk About It

Talk about the questions with your group.

1. Do you like to wear comfortable or fashionable clothes?
2. Do you like the styles today? What styles are popular right now for women? For men? Which of these styles do you like?
3. Would you like to visit Harajuku? Why or why not?

B. Role Playing

Look at the picture above. Work with a partner. One student is a salesperson. The other is a customer. Use some of the expressions below.

Salesperson: *"May I help you?" "It's on sale." "It looks good on you." "That's a nice color!"*

Customer: *"How much is this?" "This is beautiful!" "This is too expensive!" "It fits." "It's too tight." "It's too big." "It's too small."*

C. Write About It

Find a picture from a fashion magazine or the Internet. Write a short description of the picture. Use the example below.

This person is wearing a gray suit. He has a shirt and striped tie. He has short, black hair.

■ **Internet or Magazines**

What do the fashion police say? Find a website or fashion magazine showing the best- and worst-dressed actors in the last Oscars or Emmys.

■ **Television**

Watch a show about a personal makeover or home makeover. Describe how the person or home looks before and after.

■ **Make a Talk Show**

Make a talk show. Interview different people from stories in this book. Film the show and watch it in class.

■ **Movie**

Watch *Mrs. Doubtfire*. Describe the father's new look as a babysitter.

■ **In Your Journal**

Look back to the Fashion Questionnaire in Getting Ready of this unit. Write sentences about you and fashion in your journal.

■ **CNN.**

Watch the CNN® video clip for this unit.

A HARD DAY'S WORK

GETTING READY

1. Work with a partner. Look at the pictures. Match the picture to the job in the box.

___ cook	___ gardener	___ paramedic
___ teacher	___ engineer	___ administrative assistant

2. Work in a group. What does each person do in these jobs? Would you like some of these jobs? Which ones? Why?

PART ONE

THE YOUNGEST EXECUTIVE

PRE-READING

Look at the picture. Talk about the questions with your classmates.

Where is the girl?
How old is she?
What is she doing?
Why is she in a limousine?
Why is she in an office?
What does she do at the office?

Listen to your teacher. Read the story to find the answers.

THE YOUNGEST EXECUTIVE

Mary Rodas's parents came to New York from El Salvador. They lived in an apartment building. A man named Donald Spector lived in the building, too. He owned a toy company. One day Donald gave Mary a new toy. She was four years old. Mary played with the toy. She said, "This is fun!" A few weeks later Donald gave her another toy. She played with it. She said, "I don't like this toy. It doesn't work." She was an honest little girl. Donald liked her honesty, and they became friends. For years Donald gave Mary new toys, and she gave him very good ideas about the toys.

When Mary was thirteen years old, Donald showed her a new ball. The ball had a balloon inside it. Mary wanted to fill the balloon with water. She wanted to paint the ball crazy colors. She wanted to put rice or beans in it also to make it noisy. The company made these changes. Mary's ideas were a hit! The company sold thousands of the balls.

That Christmas Donald gave Mary an incredible gift. He made her a vice president of the toy company. She worked with new products at the company. Her job was to see if the new toys were fun. She had a big salary. She made $200,000 a year. In high school she took a limousine from her school to her office in New York City. She worked for three or four hours a day at her job, and then she had to do her homework. Mary was a busy teenager. She also spent time with her family. Her parents taught her that working hard and doing your best is very important.

Today Mary works at a college. She helps students make decisions about their careers. Today the little executive with bright ideas helps students think about their future.

READING AND WORD STUDY SKILLS

A. Understanding the Main Ideas

Circle the correct answer.

1. Little Mary had good ideas about new *toys / classes*.

2. Mary had good ideas about a new ball. The company sold *a lot of / a few* balls.

3. She was a *vice president / an office assistant* when she was thirteen years old.

4. Her job was to *make / play with* new toys.

5. Today Mary works at a college. She helps students with their *careers / toys*.

B. Finding Details

There is one mistake in each sentence. Correct it.

1. Mary and her family are from ~~Mexico~~ *El Salvador*.

2. Donald Spector owned an apartment building.

3. Mary was 23 years old when she was vice president.

4. Mary took a train to school.

5. Mary made $20,000 a year.

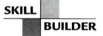

C. Making a Timeline

Making a timeline is a good way to organize information. A timeline can help you understand all the facts in a reading. It can also help you prepare to write. Complete the timeline about Mary's life.

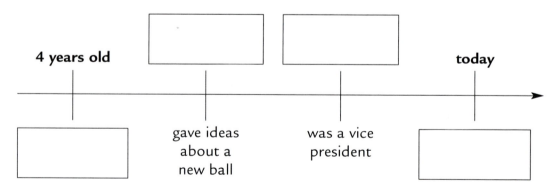

D. Learning New Words

Complete the summary with the words below.

office	products	ideas	sold
toys	salary	company	owned

Mary Rodas met Donald Spector when she was a small child. Donald
1) _____ a toy 2) _____. He asked Mary to play with
the new 3) _____. Mary gave Donald good 4) _____
about the toys.

Later she gave the company good ideas about a new ball. The company
5) _____ thousands of balls. Then Donald asked Mary to be a
vice president. Mary's job was to play with new 6) _____.
She was only in high school, but she worked in an 7) _____
and she had a big 8) _____.

Put the words above into the correct columns. Use your dictionary.

Nouns	Verbs
1.	1.
2.	2.
3.	
4.	
5.	
6.	

E. Using New Words

Find the words from exercise D in the word search.

S	C	I	R	M	Y	T	T	O	Y	S	V	R
O	O	D	H	R	O	N	I	D	E	A	S	O
L	M	R	A	Y	U	W	A	Y	R	T	Z	F
D	P	L	O	Z	W	H	N	P	L	W	D	F
Z	A	X	S	W	I	U	P	E	M	V	O	I
S	N	C	U	M	E	G	P	V	D	O	N	C
H	Y	P	R	O	D	U	C	T	S	L	C	E

COMMUNICATING YOUR IDEAS

A. Talk About It

Talk about the questions with your classmates.

1. Would you like a job like Mary's? Why or why not?
2. What toys did you play with when you were a child?
3. What games did you like to play?
4. What did you want to be when you grew up?
5. What job would you like to have now? Why?
6. What are some good jobs? Explain.
7. What are some bad jobs? Explain.

B. Write About It

Write a description of a job. The name of the job is a secret. Read your description to your classmates. They will guess the job.

Example: *I help people. I ride in a truck. I wear a yellow hat, coat and boots. I am brave. I fight fires. What am I?*

<table>
<tr><td>

PART
TWO

</td><td>

LOOKING FOR A JOB

</td></tr>
</table>

PRE-READING

1. Look at the pictures. What does Wei Lin like about her job? What doesn't she like about it?

2. Wei Lin wants a new job. Circle two ways she could find a job. Share your ideas with the class.

   sign on a store   advertisement on radio
   classified ads in the newspaper   on the Internet

3. Look at the classified ads. Circle the jobs Wei Lin might like.

Cook

Small, busy restaurant, 2 yrs exp, p/t, $10–$15/hr, no benefits. Apply in person at Little Alex's, 6756 Main St., Southgate.

Mechanic

p/t, exp, $18/hr plus benefits, will train Call 555-6655.

Office Assistant

Francisco's Furniture, general office work, f/t, good benefits, $15/hr. Computer skills, speak Spanish, very organized. Fax resume to 555-0001.

SALESPEOPLE

Busy department store.

No exp, $8-10/hr plus bonus, flexible schedule. Apply in person at 224 West Rose Ave. Richmond.

Travel Agent

Love travel? Have great customer service? Join us! F/t, will train, have computer exp., $12/h plus bonus, health benefits. E-mail resume: lewisnclark@dot.org

Glossary
f/t = full time
p/t = part time
exp = experience
yrs = years
hr = hour

READING AND WORD STUDY SKILLS

A. Finding Details

Work with a partner. Complete the chart.

Job	Experience?	F/T or P/T?	Benefits?	Pay?
cook		p/t		
office assistant			yes	
salespeople	no			
travel agent			yes	
	yes			$18/h

B. Learning New Words

full time	train	benefits
part time	experience	plus

1. Patricia needs a _____ job. She wants to work 40 hours a week.

2. Victor is a student. He only works on Saturday. He works _____.

3. _____ are things like insurance, vacation time and sick days.

4. If you did not do a job in the past, you have no _____.

5. _____ means "also" or "too."

6. _____ is similar to "teach."

C. Using New Words

Use the words above in your own sentences.

1. _____

2. _____

3. _____

4. _____

5. _____

6. _____

D. Pronouns

Look at the underlined pronoun(s). Draw a circle around the noun(s).

1. (Wei Lin) would like to get a new job. <u>She</u> does not like her job now.

2. Wei Lin does not like her manager. <u>He</u> is not kind or polite to <u>her</u>.

3. Her job is not very interesting either. In fact, <u>it</u> is boring.

4. Wei Lin's coworkers are nice. Wei Lin will miss <u>them</u> when <u>she</u> finds a new job.

E. Adjectives

Mary was an honest girl. What other adjectives do you think describe Mary? Circle them. Tell why you think so.

kind	hard-working	intelligent	helpful	polite
organized	brave	patient	creative	friendly

Write sentences about people and their jobs. Use words from the list above.

Example: *A good teacher is patient and organized.*

1. A good mechanic is _____

2. A good tour guide is _____

3. _____

4. _____

5. _____

COMMUNICATING YOUR IDEAS

A. Talk About It

What do you think about your job? Check (✓) the boxes.

My Job	Great!	Good	Okay	Bad	Terrible
the hours	☐	☐	☐	☐	☐
my salary	☐	☐	☐	☐	☐
my boss	☐	☐	☐	☐	☐
my work place	☐	☐	☐	☐	☐
my coworkers	☐	☐	☐	☐	☐
overtime pay	☐	☐	☐	☐	☐
the benefits (insurance, vacation time, sick days)	☐	☐	☐	☐	☐

Talk about jobs with a small group. Report back to the class.

1. What is your job?
2. What do you do at this job?
3. What do you like about your job?
4. What don't you like about your job?
5. Compare your answers from the chart above with your group.

B. Interviewing

Interview a native English speaker. Ask questions 1–4 from Talk About It. Report back to your class.

C. Make a Poster

Make a poster of your dream job. Write the answers to the questions below. Then draw or cut out pictures to show your ideas. Present your poster to the class.

1. What is your dream job?

2. Why do you want this job?

3. What is good about this job?

Example: *I would like to be a nurse.*

I would like this job because I like helping people.

This job has a good salary and benefits. There are many job openings. The schedule is flexible.

ONE STEP BEYOND

■ **Internet or Newspaper Search**
Look on the Internet or in your local newspaper for a job you would like. Write about why you would like it. Tell your classmates about it.

■ **Movie**
Watch the movie *Big*. Describe the boy's new job.

■ **Career Center Visit or Presentation**
Visit a career center or invite a counselor to visit your class. Learn some steps you can take toward a career you like. Write five steps you can take in your journal.

■ **In the Community**
Make an appointment to do a short interview with someone who has the job you would like. Write four questions to ask him or her. Write the answers and share them with your class.

■ **In Your Journal**
Write about what you need to do to get the job you would like.

■ **CNN.**
Watch the CNN® video clip for this unit.

be	was		**hear**	heard
become	became		**hide**	hid
begin	began		**hit**	hit
blow	blew		**keep**	kept
break	broke		**know**	knew
bring	brought		**lead**	led
build	built		**leave**	left
buy	bought		**lose**	lost
catch	caught		**make**	made
choose	chose		**meet**	met
come	came		**pay**	paid
cut	cut		**put**	put
do	did		**run**	ran
drink	drank		**say**	said
drive	drove		**see**	saw
eat	ate		**send**	sent
fall	fell		**sleep**	slept
feel	felt		**speak**	spoke
fight	fought		**spend**	spent
find	found		**take**	took
fly	flew		**teach**	taught
forget	forgot		**tell**	told
get	got		**think**	thought
give	gave		**understand**	understood
go	went		**wear**	wore
grow	grew		**win**	won
have	had		**write**	wrote

INDEX OF VOCABULARY

Heinle's Newbury House Dictionaries

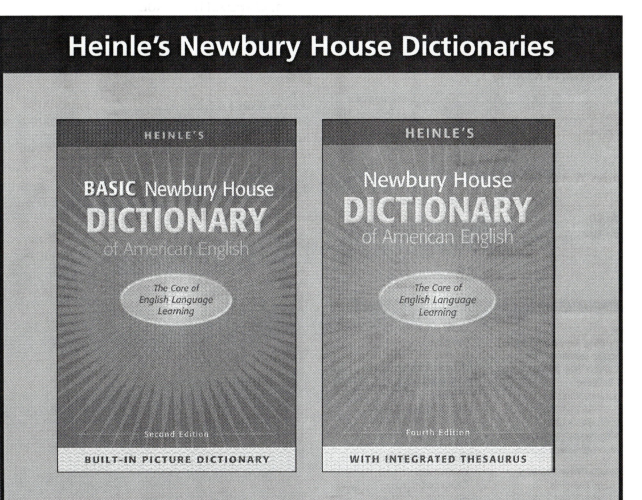

The ideal supplement for vocabulary development! Use *Heinle's Newbury House Dictionaries* to build vocabulary and increase reading skills.

Heinle's Newbury House Dictionary with Integrated Thesaurus
Softcover with CD-ROM....0-8384-2657-3
Hardcover 0-8837-7017-2

Heinle's Basic Newbury House Dictionary
Softcover 0-8384-2656-5
Hardcover 0-7593-9808-9

Heinle's Newbury House Dictionary CD-ROM (Dual Platform)
0-8384-2661-1

The Heinle Picture Dictionary
0-8384-4400-8

Stories Worth Reading Series

Stories Worth Reading 1

Text 1-4130-0853-4
Audio CD 1-4130-0854-2
Audio Tape 1-4130-0855-0

Stories Worth Reading 2

Text 1-4130-0856-9
Audio CD 1-4130-0857-7
Audio Tape 1-4130-0858-5

Video for Books 1 & 2 1-4130-1515-8
DVD for Books 1 & 2..1-4130-1826-2
Instructor's Manual for Books 1 & 2 1-4130-0859-3
Assessment CD-ROM with ExamView® Pro
   for Books 1 & 2 1-4130-1827-0

ELT INTERNATIONAL CONTACT INFORMATION

Asia
(Including Japan and India)
Cengage Learning
5 Shenton Way #01-01
UIC Building
Singapore 068808
Tel: 65-6410-1200
Fax: 65-6410-1208
info@cengagelearning.com.sg
www.cengagelearningasia.com

Australia/New Zealand
Cengage Learning
102 Dodds Street
Southbank, Victoria
Australia 3006
Tel: 03-9685-4111
Fax: 03-9685-4199
Toll Free 1-800-654-831
www.cengagelearning.com.au

Canada
Cengage Nelson
1120 Birchmount Road
Toronto, Ontario M1K 5G4
Tel: 416-752-9100
Fax: 416-752-9646
www.nelson.com

Latin America
Cengage Learning
Seneca, 53
Colonia Polanco
11560 México D.F
México
Tel: 52-55-1500-6000
Fax: 52-55-5281-2656
www.cengagelearning.com.mx

**UK/Europe/Middle
East/Africa**
Cengage Learning
High Holborn House
50/51 Bedford Row
London, WC1R 4LR
United Kingdom
Tel: 44-207-067-2500
Fax: 44-207-067-2600
www.cengagelearning.co.uk

Spain/Portugal
Cengage Paraninfo
Calle Magallanes, 25
28015 Madrid
Spain
Tel: 34-91-446-3350
Fax: 34-91-445-6218
www.paraninfo.es

For product information in the United States, desk or examination copy requests, or for the name of the Heinle Specialist in your area, call toll-free:

877-633-3375

or send requests to:
Heinle, Cengage Learning
20 Channel Center Street
Boston, MA 02210
Fax: (617) 289-7844

Examination and desk copy requests must be on school letterhead and include:

- Name
- School
- School Address with Zip Code
- Phone Number
- Enrollment
- Decision Date
- Book Title and ISBN

Please allow 3–4 weeks for delivery.

For information about:
- Placing an order
- Prices
- Availability of material
- Delivery

Call: 800-354-9706

Send orders to:
TL Distribution Center
Attn: Order Fulfillment
10650 Toebben Drive
Independence, KY 41051

PUBNET
Easy Link: 6290-5841

elt.heinle.com